IN MINUTES

Clodagh McKenna

IN MINUTES

10, 20, 30 minutes –
How much time do you have
to cook tonight?

Photography by Dora Kazmierak

Kyle Books

This book is dedicated to my husband, Harry Herbert. My moon and stars...

An Hachette UK Company
www.hachette.co.uk

First published in Great Britain in 2021
by Kyle Books, an imprint of Octopus Publishing Group Limited
Carmelite House
50 Victoria Embankment
London EC4Y 0DZ

www.kylebooks.co.uk
www.octopusbooksusa.com

ISBN: 978-1-91423-908-3

Text copyright 2021 © Clodagh McKenna
Photographs copyright 2021 © Dora Kazmierak
Design and layout copyright 2021 © Kyle Books

Distributed in the US by Hachette Book Group, 1290 Avenue of the Americas,
4th and 5th Floors, New York, NY 10104

Distributed in Canada by Canadian Manda Group, 664 Annette St., Toronto, Ontario,
Canada M6S 2C8

Publisher: Joanna Copestick
Project editor: Vicky Orchard
Editorial assistants: Jenny Dye and Zakk Raja
Design: Nikki Dupin at Studio Nic & Lou
Creative Director: Clodagh McKenna
Photography: Dora Kazmierak
Food styling: Lizzie Harris and Hanna Miller
Production: Katherine Hockley

A Cataloguing in Publication record for this title is available from the British Library

Printed and bound in China

10 9 8 7 6 5 4 3 2 1

Contents

Introduction

Over the past couple of years I feel like I have become so connected to you all whether it's via social media or ITV's *This Morning*. This connection has really shaped the way I think about food, recipes and shopping, and fitting it all in to our busy lives. The messages that you send me are always in the back of my mind when I'm creating new recipes, and for this reason I think this book will become the most used cookbook in your kitchen. I wrote it to help you cook with ease and there's no recipe in this book that anyone can't cook.

The number one topic in our messages back and forth is time, and how much or how little you may have, and how that affects your daily ability to be able to feed yourself, your family and/or friends. Every other part of our lives is timed very carefully. How long we sleep, how much time we should spend exercising, how long it takes us to get to work. But cooking... It depends on how long you've got, or how much time you are willing to spend. So that's the inspiration behind *In Minutes*. Each section is carefully curated with easy recipes using accessible ingredients and that you can cook in either 10, 20 or 30 minutes.

The book comprises 80 recipes that will soon (I hope!) be your weekly staples, from Warm Lentil Salad with Goat's Cheese to a Thai Red Curry and Chicken Katsu Ramen. There are vegan and vegetarian recipes and I've given options for alternative ingredients in the Recipe Swaps so you can use whatever you have in your cupboards or turn a meal into a vegan or veggie option.

Introduction

The book is divided into three chapters based on time to make it as user-friendly as possible:

- **10-minute recipes** – speedy salads to make you glow, pastas for the whole family and no-stress noodles

- **20-minute recipes** – light and crispy tempuras, spicy curries for vegans and vegetarians alike, and single-serve ramens

- **30-minute recipes** – healthy fish dishes, delicious tarts, mouth-watering burgers and one-pot chicken suppers

I cook at home every night; I believe I am worth it and that you're worth it too. It makes you feel good both mentally and physically, there's no doubt in the world about that. You wake up in the morning feeling better having cooked a homemade meal, people feel loved when someone has prepared a plate of food for them, and it's way less expensive than pre-prepared foods and takeaways. Time is what holds us all back. This book will make it easier for you – some nights you may have 10 minutes and other nights half an hour, so there's a recipe in here for whatever kind of day you might be having.

Don't stress yourself out or mentally beat yourself up about not putting on a lavish meal every night of the week (no one wants that anyway!). Simple dishes like my Rapid Salmon Ramen (page 44) or The Tuna Express (page 47) or a big bowl of comforting, fragrant dahl (page 34) can all be made in 10 minutes and will make you feel your good ol' self again, no matter what the day threw at you.

My big wish is that this book brings you happiness, passion, tools and ideas to help you enjoy a home-cooked meal every night.

Love and happiness
Clo xx

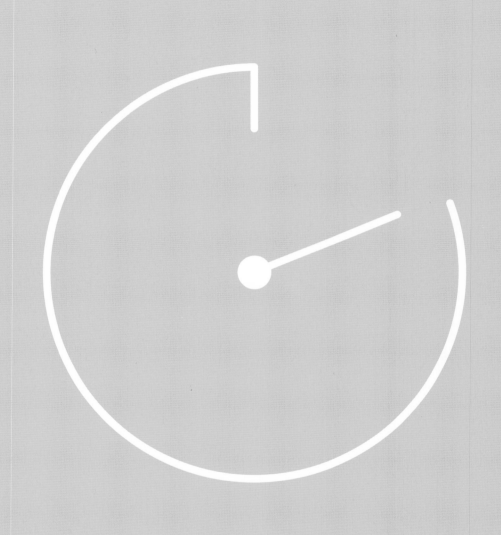

10
Minutes

Cloglow Salad

10 MINS / **SERVES 4**

I love the feeling that I get from eating this salad – it makes me feel hydrated, cared for, energetic, happy and also gives me an inner glow that feeds my outer glow! I sometimes swap out the red cabbage for grated carrots, or the kale for spinach, or the broccoli for French beans.

50g (1¾oz) pumpkin seeds

50g (1¾oz) walnuts, roughly chopped

200g (7oz) sprouting broccoli, cut into chunks

150g (5½oz) frozen edamame beans

250g (9oz) packet of pre-cooked quinoa

60g (2¼oz) kale, shredded

60g (2¼oz) red cabbage, finely shredded

1 ripe avocado, diced

2 cooked beetroot, diced

60g (2¼oz) pomegranate seeds

60g (2¼oz) mixed sprouted seeds and lentils

For the citrus dressing

zest and juice of 1 orange

zest and juice of 1 lemon

1 tablespoon apple cider vinegar

1 teaspoon raw honey

2 tablespoons extra virgin olive oil

1 teaspoon Dijon mustard

sea salt and freshly ground black pepper

1. Place the pumpkin seeds and walnuts in a frying pan and dry toast over a medium heat for 2 minutes, stirring every so often, until they smell toasted and the pumpkin seeds are starting to pop.

2. Meanwhile, blanch the broccoli in a pan of salted boiling water for 3 minutes, adding the edamame beans for the final minute of cooking. Drain and plunge into ice-cold water to stop them cooking. Once cold, drain again.

3. Make your dressing by combining all the ingredients and whisking well. Season to taste.

4. To assemble the salad, place all the ingredients in a large bowl, add the dressing and toss together.

 Baby spinach, cavolo nero or any other dark, leafy green would be a great, healthy addition. The walnuts and pumpkin seeds can be substituted for whatever nuts and seeds you have to hand.

10 Minutes

Warm Lentil Salad with Goat's Cheese

How gorgeous does this salad look?! Made from lentils that you can store in your cupboard (a good staple to have in there), and livened up with juicy, sweet beetroot, sharp chicory, creamy goat's cheese and vibrant fresh herbs. It's a really filling salad, which is super healthy and a no-fuss, no-stress supper.

10 MINS / **SERVES 2**

1 tablespoon olive oil

1 garlic clove, crushed

½ tablespoon finely chopped rosemary

250g (9oz) packet of pre-cooked Puy lentils

2 cooked beetroot, halved and cut into wedges

½ radicchio, roughly torn

50g (1¾oz) soft goat's cheese, broken into large chunks

50g (1¾oz) pecans

1 tablespoon flat-leaf parsley, roughly chopped

1 tablespoon mint, roughly chopped

sea salt and freshly ground black pepper

For the dressing

1 tablespoon sherry vinegar

1 tablespoon maple syrup

2 tablespoons extra virgin olive oil

1. Heat the oil in a medium pan over a medium heat, add the garlic and rosemary and gently fry until the garlic is just turning a light golden colour. Stir in the lentils and warm through. Season to taste.

2. To make the dressing, whisk all the ingredients together and season with salt and pepper.

3. Toss the dressing, beetroot and torn radicchio leaves through the warm lentil mixture and transfer to a serving dish.

4. Scatter over the goat's cheese, pecans, parsley and mint and serve.

 Torn mozzarella or burrata or crumbled vegan feta cheese are good alternatives for the goat's cheese.

Taco Salad

10 MINS / **SERVES 2**

This salad is bursting with bold, satisfying Tex-Mex flavours and layers of fresh, creamy, crunchy textures. It's so easy to pull together as it's full of common, pantry-friendly taco ingredients – canned black beans and sweetcorn, crisp lettuce, juicy tomatoes and creamy avocados – so you can make it at a moment's notice. You can even make it ahead and just add the tortilla chips at the last minute.

400g (14oz) can of black beans, drained and rinsed

200g (7oz) can of sweetcorn, drained

2 medium tomatoes, diced

1 ripe avocado, diced

½ red onion, finely sliced

1 baby gem lettuce, shredded

1 tablespoon olive oil

juice of 1 lime

a small handful of coriander, roughly chopped

30g (1oz) Cheddar cheese, grated

30g (1oz) tortilla chips, roughly broken

sea salt and freshly ground black pepper

1. In a large bowl, combine the black beans, sweetcorn, tomatoes, avocado, onion and lettuce. Add the olive oil and lime juice. Toss together and season to taste.

2. Scatter over the coriander, grated Cheddar and tortilla chips just before serving.

10 Minutes

Grilled Vegetable & Couscous Salad

This salad is brilliant when you want a big hit of vegetables and something that will satisfy a hunger too. I sometimes mix in ½ teaspoon of harissa paste with the olive oil if I want a fiery kick. Or if I am feeling extra hungry, I add a can of drained and rinsed chickpeas or butter beans. Feta, ricotta or goat's cheese are delicious with it too!

10 MINS / **SERVES 2**

100g (3½oz) couscous

100ml (3½fl oz) hot vegetable stock

1 small green or yellow courgette, thinly sliced lengthwise

1 tablespoon extra virgin olive oil, plus extra for grilling

10 cherry tomatoes, quartered

50g (1¾oz) semi-dried tomatoes

1 roasted red pepper from a jar, deseeded and roughly chopped

100g (3½oz) chargrilled artichokes, cut into bite-sized chunks

10 pitted green olives, roughly chopped

2 tablespoons flat-leaf parsley roughly chopped

juice of 1 lemon

sea salt and freshly ground black pepper

1. Put the couscous in a large bowl. Pour over the hot vegetable stock and cover with clingfilm. Leave for 4 minutes until all the stock has been absorbed, then fluff up with a fork.

2. Meanwhile, heat a griddle pan over a high heat. Brush the courgette slices with oil, season with salt and grill for 2 minutes on each side or until nicely charred and just cooked.

3. Once the couscous is ready, add all the remaining ingredients, toss well and season to taste.

 You can use aubergines instead of the courgettes if you wish. Mint and coriander leaves would also be delicious with or without the flat-leaf parsley. Grilled chicken or prawns can be added if you want to make it a more substantial meal.

Lemony Fettuccine Alfredo

This dish is insanely good! And it couldn't be easier to whip up after a long day's work... The whispers of lemon swimming through the cream, rich butter, salty caramel Parmesan and peppery flat-leaf parsley make it one of the best pasta recipes I have ever made. I promise that you'll be licking your plate and it will become one of your go-to quick suppers.

10 MINS / **SERVES 4**

500g (1lb 2oz) fresh fettuccine
500ml (18fl oz) double cream
1 unwaxed lemon, thinly sliced
1 garlic clove
110g (4oz) butter, cut into small pieces
75g (2¾oz) freshly grated Parmesan cheese, plus extra to serve
a grating of fresh nutmeg
1 tablespoon flat-leaf parsley, chopped
sea salt and freshly ground black pepper

1. Place a large saucepan of salted water over a high heat and bring to the boil. Stir in the fettuccine and cook for 5 minutes.

2. While the pasta is cooking, place a deep frying pan or saucepan over a low–medium heat. Pour in the cream and add the lemon slices and garlic clove. Next, add the butter and whisk gently until melted. Remove and discard the garlic. Stir in the grated Parmesan and nutmeg. Season with freshly ground black pepper.

3. Drain the pasta, reserving a cup of the pasta cooking water. Add the pasta to the pan of Alfredo sauce and gently toss to coat it in the sauce.

4. Top the pasta with more grated Parmesan and chopped flat-leaf parsley to serve.

 You could add crispy pancetta to the pasta sauce, and use linguine or spaghetti instead of the fettuccine.

10 Minutes

Spring Garden Gnocchi

This spring green vegetable gnocchi has all the flavours I love about spring in one bowl. It's light and fresh and a quick and easy weeknight meal that will boost your vegetable intake, and feed that longing for a delicious supper after a long day. I use frozen peas and baby spinach, but you can also use purple sprouting broccoli, asparagus or chard.

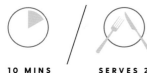

10 MINS / SERVES 2

20g (¾oz) butter
50g (1¾oz) baby spinach
80g (2¾oz) frozen peas, defrosted
2 tablespoons fresh basil pesto
2 tablespoons full-fat crème fraîche
300g (10½oz) gnocchi
a handful of basil leaves
sea salt and freshly ground black pepper

1. Place a large frying pan over a medium heat and add the butter. Once the butter has melted, stir in the baby spinach and peas. Cook for 1 minute until the spinach has wilted. Stir in the basil pesto and crème fraîche, then reduce the heat and cook for 2 minutes.

2. Meanwhile, cook the gnocchi in a pan of salted boiling water according to the packet instructions, then scoop out with a slotted spoon into the frying pan. Season with salt and pepper. Toss everything together and serve with a sprinkle of basil leaves.

You can substitute the crème fraîche with 100ml (3½fl oz) double cream. You could also swap the peas for cooked asparagus cut into 2.5cm (1in) pieces.

Creamy Forest Pasta

10 MINS / **SERVES 4**

If it's chilly outside, you've had a long day and come home to hungry faces, then this is what you should make. A big-flavoured, comforting pasta that is so stress-free you'll be dancing while you make it (that you should definitely do!). If you don't have wild mushrooms, don't worry, I have a list of substitutes below. Now get that wine poured and whip up this dish in under 10 minutes!

600g (1lb 5oz) fresh tagliatelle
60g (2¼oz) toasted hazelnuts, roughly chopped

For the wild mushroom sauce
1 tablespoon olive oil
1 tablespoon butter
400g (14oz) mixed wild mushrooms, sliced
2 garlic cloves, crushed
1 tablespoon chopped rosemary, plus extra to serve
100ml (3½fl oz) white wine
200g (7oz) full-fat crème fraîche
sea salt and freshly ground black pepper

1. To make the wild mushroom sauce, heat the oil and butter in a large, heavy-bottomed pan over a high heat. Add the mushrooms and fry for 4 minutes.

2. While the mushrooms are frying, cook the tagliatelle in a large saucepan of salted boiling water according to the packet instructions. Drain, reserving a couple of tablespoons of the cooking water.

3. Once the mushrooms are nice and golden, add the garlic and rosemary and fry for 30 seconds until aromatic. Pour in the white wine and reduce the heat to medium. Cook for a further minute, stirring well, until the wine has reduced. Fold through the crème fraîche, season with salt and pepper and simmer for 2 minutes.

4. Return the tagliatelle to the large saucepan. Add the reserved pasta cooking water and the mushroom sauce, mix well and serve with the hazelnuts scattered over the top and a sprinkling of chopped rosemary.

Supermarkets often sell punnets of mixed, wild mushrooms (sometimes called 'woodland' mushrooms) but if you can't find these, then any combination of chestnut mushrooms, oyster mushrooms, portobello or fresh shiitake works well.

Fusilli with Walnut & Kale Pesto

Peppery, nutty and creamy textures and flavours oozing into pasta. I am using fusilli here but you could use any kind of pasta you have to hand. Swap out the kale for flat-leaf parsley or basil if you prefer.

10 MINS / **SERVES 2**

300g (10½oz) fresh fusilli
75g (2¾oz) kale, chopped
60g (2¼oz) walnuts, plus extra
  to serve
a small bunch of basil leaves
2 garlic cloves
120ml (4fl oz) extra virgin olive oil
50g (1¾oz) Parmesan cheese,
  grated, plus extra to serve
150g (5½oz) ricotta
sea salt and freshly ground black
  pepper

1. Cook the fusilli in a large pan of salted boiling water according to the packet instructions. Drain and set aside.

2. Meanwhile, in a separate pan of salted boiling water, blanch the kale for 1 minute. Drain and rinse under cold water until cool.

3. Put the kale, walnuts, basil and garlic in a food processor and pulse until chopped. Add the olive oil and Parmesan and pulse until combined but not completely smooth. Season to taste.

4. Toss the fusilli and kale pesto together, then crumble over the ricotta and stir in. Serve with a final showering of grated Parmesan and a few walnuts crumbled over the top.

 You can use hazelnuts, almonds or pine nuts instead of the walnuts. Penne and paccheri pasta are great alternatives to fusilli. For a gluten-free option, just use gluten-free pasta.

Topped Flatbreads Four Ways

10 MINS / **SERVES 2**

Topped flatbreads are so fun to make and are like an express homemade pizza! Here are four different ways to create a super simple delicious topping. I have a stack of flatbreads in my freezer, so they are always on hand and are brilliant for using up the leftovers from the weekend on a Monday night!

Courgette, Tomato, Pine Nut & Red Pesto Flatbread

2 large garlic flatbreads
80g (2¾oz) fresh red pesto
1 medium courgette, cut into thick ribbons using a vegetable peeler
80g (2¾oz) sun-dried tomatoes in oil, drained and roughly chopped
2 tablespoons pine nuts
sea salt and freshly ground black pepper

1. Preheat the oven to 200°C/400°F/gas mark 6.

2. Place the flatbreads on a lined baking tray, spread over the red pesto and scatter over the courgette ribbons. Dot over the sun-dried tomatoes, scatter over the pine nuts and bake for 8–9 minutes.

3. Season well and serve.

Pesto, Spinach & Ricotta Flatbread

½ tablespoon butter
60g (2¼oz) baby spinach
2 large, thick flatbreads
100g (3½oz) fresh basil pesto
200g (7oz) ricotta
a grating of fresh nutmeg
½ teaspoon chilli flakes
sea salt and freshly ground black pepper

1. Preheat the oven to 200°C/400°F/gas mark 6.

2. Melt the butter in a small frying pan over a medium heat. Add the spinach and sauté for 1 minute until just wilted. Remove to a kitchen-paper-lined plate and blot well to remove any excess liquid. Lay the flatbreads on a lined baking tray and spread over the pesto.

3. Cover with the spinach and dot teaspoonfuls of ricotta over the top. Season liberally with salt and pepper, a grating of nutmeg and the chilli flakes. Bake for 5 minutes.

Roasted Red Pepper, Hummus, Burrata & Tomato Flatbread

2 large, thick flatbreads

120g (4½oz) hummus

10 cherry tomatoes, halved

2 large roasted red peppers from a jar, deseeded and sliced

1 medium burrata

a drizzle of extra virgin olive oil

1 tablespoon basil leaves, torn

sea salt and freshly ground black pepper

1. Heat a griddle pan over a high heat and grill the flatbreads for 1 minute on each side or until they have nice grill marks.

2. Spread a thick layer of hummus over each flatbread and scatter over the cherry tomatoes and red peppers.

3. Tear the burrata into bite-sized chunks and dot around the flatbread.

4. Season liberally, drizzle over a good glug of extra virgin olive oil and scatter over the torn basil leaves.

Greek Gyros

1 tablespoon olive oil

1 large garlic clove, grated

175g (6oz) cooked chicken breast, torn into shreds

1 teaspoon dried oregano

2 large, thick pitta breads

100g (3½oz) tzatziki

¼ cucumber, deseeded and grated

1 tomato, sliced

a large handful of lettuce, shredded

½ red onion, thinly sliced

sea salt and freshly ground black pepper

1. Heat the oil in a non-stick frying pan over a medium heat. Add half the garlic and fry for 30 seconds. Add the chicken and oregano and fry for 2 minutes until hot. Season liberally.

2. Warm the pitta breads under a hot grill for 1–2 minutes. Spread with a good layer of tzatziki, top with the cucumber, tomato, lettuce and red onion and scatter over the warm chicken.

The Dahl Deal

10 MINS / **SERVES 2**

A delicious golden bowl of heaven! Transporting you to India in one single spoonful. The aromatic spices infusing the lentils, chickpeas and coconut milk are utterly delicious. So many of these ingredients are from the storecupboard, so this is a really easy supper to make fast without fuss. You can also add frozen peas, French beans or chopped cauliflower. Serve it up on its own or with some naan for scooping.

1 tablespoon vegetable oil
½ green chilli, chopped
1 teaspoon cumin seeds
3 garlic cloves, grated
2cm (¾in) piece of fresh ginger,
   peeled and grated
1 teaspoon ground turmeric
1 teaspoon mild curry powder
2 plum tomatoes, roughly chopped
1 teaspoon salt
300ml (10fl oz) coconut milk
400g (14oz) can of chickpeas,
   drained and rinsed
400g (14oz) can of red lentils,
   drained and rinsed
80g (2¾oz) baby spinach
1 tablespoon coriander,
   roughly chopped

1. Heat the oil in a large, ovenproof casserole dish or saucepan over a medium heat. Add the chopped chilli, cumin seeds, garlic and ginger and fry for 30 seconds until fragrant. Add the turmeric and curry powder and fry for a further 30 seconds.

2. Add the chopped tomatoes, salt, coconut milk, chickpeas and lentils and simmer rapidly for 7–8 minutes.

3. Using the back of a wooden spoon crush about a quarter of the dahl against the side of the pan to break down some of the chickpeas and lentils. This will thicken the sauce.

4. Stir through the baby spinach until wilted. Season to taste, scatter over the coriander and serve.

 Any mix of canned red kidney beans, borlotti beans or cannellini beans works as a substitute for either the chickpeas or lentils.

One & Yum Squid

10 MINS / **SERVES 4**

I think squid is one of those ingredients you see on the fish counter and think, 'I'd like to cook it, but I'm not sure how'. Am I right?! Well, you either cook squid fast or slow, that's the rule, otherwise it gets chewy. And this book is all about fast, delicious quick fixes, so it's perfect for that kind of cooking! With spicy chorizo, earthy chickpeas, peppery kale and crunchy almonds, this dish feels like an instant taste-escape to Spain, but from the comfort of your own home. Glass of Chablis, anyone?

3 tablespoons extra virgin olive oil

225g (8oz) cooking chorizo, sliced

3 garlic cloves, crushed

½ teaspoon chilli flakes

500g (1lb 2oz) squid, cleaned and cut into 1.5cm (⅝in) rings, tentacles halved

2 x 400g (14oz) cans of chickpeas, drained and rinsed

100g (3½oz) kale, roughly chopped

50g (1¾oz) flaked almonds, toasted

sea salt and freshly ground black pepper

1. Heat the oil in a large frying pan over a medium heat. Add the sliced chorizo and fry for 2 minutes. Stir in the garlic and chilli flakes and fry for 30 seconds.

2. Add the squid and stir-fry for 1 minute before stirring through the chickpeas and kale. Cook for a further minute until the chickpeas are warmed through and the kale has wilted.

3. Season to taste and serve with the toasted almonds scattered over the top.

Swap in shelled king prawns or diced cod for the squid. For a shellfish-free version, substitute diced chicken thighs and stir-fry until cooked through before adding the chickpeas and kale.

10 Minutes

Gambas Pil Pil

10 MINS / SERVES 4

Gambas pil pil is what I cook when I want a burst of juicy, fiery flavours! It's a quick and easy traditional tapas recipe made with fresh prawns cooked very quickly in good-quality olive oil, garlic and chilli and served sizzling, on toasted sourdough bread. I use chilli flakes because I always have them in my storecupboard, but you can use fresh chillies if you have them to hand.

100ml (3½fl oz) olive oil

4 garlic cloves, thinly sliced

1 tablespoon chilli flakes

24 fresh raw prawns, peeled

juice of 1 lemon, plus 1 lemon, cut into 4 wedges to serve

2 tablespoons flat-leaf parsley, finely chopped

4 slices of sourdough bread

sea salt and freshly ground black pepper

1. Place a frying pan over a medium heat and pour in half the olive oil. Next, stir in the garlic and chilli flakes and cook for 1 minute, then tip in the raw prawns. Season with salt and pepper, toss and cook for 1 minute on each side until they just turn pink. Pour in the lemon juice and sprinkle over the chopped flat-leaf parsley, while still over the high heat, and toss well.

2. Toast or griddle the sliced sourdough bread and divide between four dishes. Drizzle the remaining olive oil over the toast, then spoon the prawns on top, scooping up all the juices from the pan and drizzling over. Serve with a wedge of lemon.

Flatbreads work really well too if you want to swap them for the sourdough. Lime is just as delicious as lemon if you prefer its flavour.

Moroccan Prawn Rice Bowl

10 MINS / **SERVES 2**

It's amazing that in just 10 minutes you can make this bowl that is jumping with flavours. I use pre-cooked rice in this recipe which makes it super fast to throw together. The harissa paste is a must for your storecupboard, you can pick it up in any supermarket – it adds chilli, garlic and smoky flavours in just one spoonful!

1 tablespoon olive oil

180g (6oz) large, raw prawns

4 spring onions, sliced thinly

1 garlic clove, crushed

2 teaspoons harissa paste

½ teaspoon ground turmeric

200g (7oz) canned chickpeas, drained and rinsed

250g (9oz) packet of pre-cooked, microwave brown basmati rice

1 tablespoon chopped flat-leaf parsley

juice of 1 lemon

sea salt and freshly ground black pepper

1. Place a frying pan over a medium heat and add the olive oil. Add the raw prawns, spring onions and garlic, season with salt and pepper and cook for 2 minutes – tossing every 30 seconds.

2. Once the prawns turn pink, stir in the harissa and turmeric and cook for 1 minute. Next, add the chickpeas and rice and cook for about 3 minutes until heated through. Stir in the flat-leaf parsley and a squeeze of lemon juice, to taste.

You can use grilled halloumi or chicken as a substitute for the prawns.

10 Minutes

Linguine Puttanesca

10 MINS / **SERVES 2**

I love that an Italian named this dish after a – how do I put this so that I don't offend anyone? – a lady of the night, selling love for money. You get the idea! The pasta is hot and fiery, and so addictive, I guess that's how it got its name. If you aren't a fan of anchovies, I get it. Neither am I usually, but I love them in this sauce. If you're not convinced, then just add an extra tablespoon of capers instead.

200g (7oz) linguine

2 tablespoons olive oil

200g (7oz) canned cherry tomatoes

2 garlic cloves, crushed

4 anchovy fillets, roughly chopped

1 teaspoon chilli flakes

1 tablespoon capers, rinsed

12 black olives, pitted and chopped

a handful of basil leaves

sea salt and freshly ground black pepper

1. Cook the linguine in a large pan of salted boiling water for 9 minutes or until the pasta is cooked. Drain and reserve half a cup of the pasta cooking water.

2. While the pasta is cooking, place a frying pan over a medium heat and add the olive oil. Stir in the tomatoes and a pinch of salt and cook over a high heat for 2–3 minutes, stirring often. Stir in the garlic, anchovies and chilli flakes. Reduce the heat to low and cook for 3 minutes. Stir in the capers and olives and cook for a further minute. Add the cooked linguine and reserved pasta cooking water to the sauce and stir well.

3. Divide the linguine puttanesca between two bowls, season with pepper and tear over the basil leaves just before serving.

Use spaghetti instead of the linguine.

Rapid Salmon Ramen

10 MINS / **SERVES 1**

Some of you might remember me cooking this on ITV's *This Morning* where I cook every week. It's my go-to dish when I want a warm bowl of something healing, comforting and also guilt-free, that I can make in 10 minutes. I use the miso mix that comes in a packet with the noodles just because I don't really use miso in anything else – but if you do then you can just use ramen noodles and add 1 teaspoon of miso paste. Add whatever green vegetables you want – I've included a list of suggestions below for you.

1 tablespoon olive oil
1 salmon fillet, weighing 240g (8½oz)
204g (7oz) miso ramen noodle pack
¾ teaspoon chilli flakes
3 slices of fresh ginger, peeled
2 pak choi, quartered lengthways
3 sprigs of coriander
sea salt and freshly ground black pepper

1. Preheat the oven to 200°C/400°F/gas mark 6.

2. Start by cooking the salmon. Place a frying pan over a medium heat and add the olive oil. Once the pan is hot, place the salmon in the pan, skin-side down, and season with salt and pepper. Turn the salmon after 1 minute, then cook for a further minute and transfer to the oven to cook for 8 minutes.

3. If using a ready-made miso ramen pack, like I do, then place the noodles, chilli flakes, sliced ginger and ramen mix in a saucepan and pour 300ml (10fl oz) boiling water over the top. Alternatively, you can whisk 1 teaspoon of miso paste into the boiling water with one serving of ramen noodles. Place the pan over a medium heat and stir. Add the pak choi and cook for 3 minutes.

4. Pour all the ingredients into a bowl and place the cooked salmon on top. Sprinkle the coriander on top and enjoy!

Choose from: spinach, spring onions, shredded cabbage, peas, baby kale, purple sprouting broccoli or sliced mushrooms.

Instead of salmon try shredded leftover roast pork, chicken or lamb. Tofu, prawns, soft-boiled eggs or meaty fish, such as hake or cod, all work well, too.

10 Minutes

The Tuna Express

 /

10 MINS / **SERVES 2**

Step on board for a journey of bouncing flavours! The peppery, tangy flavours coating the borlotti bean salad act as the canvas to this dish. Topped with flash-cooked melting tuna and finished with a sweet, salty, peppery salsa verde. My kind of express supper that feels like such a treat for the senses and is also super healthy – hooray!

2 tuna steaks, about 2cm (¾in) thick
1 tablespoon olive oil
sea salt and freshly ground black pepper

For the borlotti bean salad
400g (14oz) can of borlotti beans, drained and rinsed
10 cherry tomatoes, quartered
1 tablespoon flat-leaf parsley, chopped
1 tablespoon red wine vinegar
1 tablespoon extra virgin olive oil

For the salsa verde
1 tablespoon red wine vinegar
4 sprigs of basil
2 sprigs of flat-leaf parsley
2 garlic cloves, crushed
1 tablespoon capers
200ml (7fl oz) extra virgin olive oil

1. Start by making the bean salad. Place the borlotti beans and tomatoes in a bowl. Add the parsley, vinegar and oil. Toss together and season to taste.

2. To make the salsa verde, place all the ingredients in a food processor and blend for 1 minute.

3. Heat a heavy cast-iron or griddle pan over a medium heat until smoking hot. Brush each tuna steak all over with the olive oil and season liberally with salt and pepper. Sear the tuna for a minute on each side.

4. Cut the tuna steaks into slices, drizzle over the salsa verde and serve with the bean salad.

 Switch the tuna for any meaty fish, such as salmon, cod or hake. For a vegetarian alternative, try portobello mushrooms or thick slices of halloumi.

Nutty Chicken

Delicious, chargrilled pieces of chicken, coated in an addictive peanut sauce that takes just 5 minutes to make! I love serving this with coconut rice as it partners so well with the satay flavours. See the Recipe Swap for alternatives to the chicken.

10 MINS / **SERVES 2**

4 skinless, boneless chicken thigh
  fillets, cut into strips
½ cucumber, diced
1 tablespoon white wine vinegar
1 tablespoon caster sugar
250g (9oz) packet of pre-cooked,
  microwave coconut rice
½ small red onion, sliced
pinch of chilli flakes

For the marinade

1 tablespoon peanut oil
¾ teaspoon ground turmeric
½ teaspoon mild curry powder
1 garlic clove, grated
1 teaspoon caster sugar
½ teaspoon salt

For the peanut satay sauce

165ml (5½fl oz) can of coconut milk
4 tablespoons crunchy peanut
  butter
juice of ½ lime
½ teaspoon lemongrass paste
1cm (½in) piece of fresh ginger,
  peeled and grated
½ tablespoon mild curry powder
½ tablespoon dark soft brown
  sugar
1 tablespoon light soy sauce

1. First, make the peanut satay sauce. Place all the ingredients in a small saucepan over a medium heat and simmer for 5 minutes.

2. Meanwhile, put the chicken thighs in a glass bowl, add the marinade ingredients and mix well until the thighs are evenly coated.

3. Heat a griddle pan until smoking hot. Place the marinated chicken in the pan and cook for 3 minutes on each side, or until cooked through.

4. While the chicken is cooking, combine the cucumber, white wine vinegar and caster sugar in a small bowl and cook the coconut rice according to the packet instructions.

5. Serve the satay on the coconut rice with the cucumber salad, sliced red onion, a sprinkle of chilli flakes and the peanut sauce drizzled over the top.

Thin strips of pork fillet work really well with satay sauce or, for a meat-free alternative, substitute thick slices of firm tofu.

Express Stir-fried Rice with Pancetta & Peas

A good stir-fried rice is such a great recipe to know by heart, as it's a brilliant way to whip up any leftover rice from the night before into a delicious, easy supper. I have added smoky, crispy pancetta and frozen peas (as I always have both in my freezer), but you can add any green vegetables that you want – sliced broccoli, green beans, kale, the list goes on! The ultimate express supper for when you feel like you just can't bear the idea of cooking tonight…

10 MINS / SERVES 2

1½ tablespoons vegetable oil

2 large eggs, beaten

200g (7oz) pancetta lardons

4 spring onions, sliced

2 garlic cloves, crushed

1cm (½in) piece of fresh ginger, peeled and grated

½ teaspoon chilli flakes

300g (10½oz) leftover cooked rice or pre-cooked, microwave basmati rice

2 teaspoons toasted sesame oil

3 tablespoons light soy sauce

350g (12oz) frozen peas

1. Heat 1 tablespoon of vegetable oil in a wok until hot. Add the beaten eggs and scramble for 2 minutes or until just cooked. Remove to a plate and set aside.

2. Add the remaining vegetable oil to the pan and throw in the pancetta and spring onions. Stir-fry for 2 minutes over a high heat until the pancetta is starting to turn crispy. Add the garlic, ginger and chilli flakes and fry for 30 seconds before adding the rice, sesame oil, soy sauce and 2 tablespoons of water. Fry for 3 minutes, stirring constantly to break up any clumps of rice and to combine everything well.

3. Add the frozen peas and mix until they are warmed through. Fold through the scrambled egg and serve.

Sliced bacon, ham, shredded cooked chicken or small cooked prawns are good alternatives. For a veggie version, try smoked tofu cut into cubes or add another egg or two.

10 Minutes

Egg & Sausage Muffin

This is one is for my friends who are fans of fast-food joints. I decided to experiment with creating a homemade version with delicious juicy sausage meat from the butcher peppered with fresh sage and aromatic nutmeg, teamed with melting mature Cheddar cheese sandwiched in floury English muffins. Yes, it's sensational!

10 MINS / **SERVES 4**

400g (14oz) sausage meat
½ tablespoon sage, finely chopped
a pinch of freshly grated nutmeg
2 tablespoons olive oil, plus extra
  for brushing (optional)
4 slices of mature Cheddar cheese
4 English muffins, cut in half and
  toasted
4 eggs
sea salt and freshly ground black
  pepper

1. First, make the sausage patties. In a large bowl, combine the sausage meat, sage and nutmeg. Season liberally and mix everything together thoroughly. Divide the mixture into four, shape into balls and then flatten into patties, just slightly larger than the English muffins.

2. Heat 1 tablespoon of olive oil in a large frying pan. Add the sausage patties and fry for 3 minutes on each side. For the final minute of cooking, place a cheese slice on top of each patty to melt.

3. While the sausage patties are cooking, heat the remaining 1 tablespoon of oil in another frying pan, crack in the eggs and cook to your liking. If you would prefer round eggs that fit the muffins exactly, brush four egg rings liberally with oil and place in the pan. Crack an egg into each ring. Add 2 tablespoons of water to the pan and quickly cover with a lid. Cook for 1–2 minutes or until the eggs are cooked to your liking.

4. Build your sandwich by topping the four muffin halves with the cheese-covered patties, eggs, a sprinkling of salt and pepper and the tops of the muffins.

 For a quick alternative to the sausage patties, substitute 2 slices of grilled bacon per muffin. For a vegetarian version, take 4 vegetarian sausages and slice each one into three lengthways before pan-frying for 3 minutes on each side.

10 Minutes

Ham, Gruyère & Spinach Quesadilla

This is an upgraded toastie, let's be honest, but sometimes that's all you want! The quesadilla gets deliciously crunchy with the oozing Gruyère, ham and leafy spinach all melting together – easy, fast and oh so good!

10 MINS / **SERVES 1**

½ tablespoon wholegrain mustard
2 large flour tortilla wraps
80g (2¾oz) Gruyère cheese, grated
2 thick slices of ham, cut into bite-sized pieces
a large handful of baby spinach, roughly chopped
1 tablespoon olive oil
freshly ground black pepper

1. Spread the wholegrain mustard over one of the tortillas. Scatter over half the Gruyère, followed by the ham and baby spinach.

2. Scatter over the remaining cheese, season with pepper and top with the other tortilla.

3. Heat ¼ tablespoon of olive oil in a large frying pan over a medium heat. Add the quesadilla and fry for 2–3 minutes, checking that the underside does not burn. Brush the top of the quesadilla with the remaining olive oil, then flip and fry for a further 2–3 minutes until the cheese has melted and the tortillas are crispy and golden.

4. Transfer to a chopping board and slice into wedges to serve.

 Use grated Cheddar, Comté or Jarlsberg cheese if you don't have Gruyère.

Poached Eggs in 'Nduja Tomato Sauce with Butter Beans

If you haven't tasted 'nduja before, now is the time! It's a delicious, very spicy, spreadable pork sausage from Calabria in Italy that you can buy in a jar and store in your fridge (once opened). Add to a rich tomato passata along with garlic, cumin and smoked paprika to create an amazing, spicy, rich tomato sauce that you can make it just a few minutes. A runny egg on top, with butter beans, make it more a substantial supper.

10 MINS / **SERVES 2**

1 tablespoon olive oil

2 tablespoons 'nduja

1 garlic clove, crushed

½ teaspoon ground cumin

½ teaspoon smoked paprika, plus extra to serve

150g (5½oz) tomato passata

1 teaspoon balsamic vinegar

2 large eggs

400g (14oz) can of butter beans, drained and rinsed

1 tablespoon flat-leaf parsley, chopped

sea salt and freshly ground black pepper

1. Heat the olive oil in a medium saucepan over a medium heat. Add the 'nduja and fry for 1 minute, breaking it up with a spoon as it cooks. Add the garlic and fry for 30 seconds until fragrant. Add the spices and stir together for a further 30 seconds. Pour in the tomato passata and balsamic vinegar, stir well and simmer for 5 minutes.

2. Meanwhile, poach the eggs in boiling water for 4 minutes.

3. Add the butter beans to the tomato sauce, stir through to warm and season to taste.

4. Spoon the beans into two bowls, top with a poached egg and finish with a sprinkle of smoked paprika and salt and scatter over the parsley.

RECIPE SWAP

If you can't find 'nduja, then substitute diced cooking chorizo. For a vegetarian alternative, add ½ teaspoon of chilli flakes to the tomato sauce instead of the 'nduja.

Our House Favourite Carbonara

10 MINS / **SERVES 4**

I could make this carbonara with my eyes closed (sometimes they are!). After a long day filming on ITV's *This Morning* or writing up recipes, I crave this creamy, smoky, peppery dish. Here's how the evening goes: I get everything prepped ahead, then I take my glass of wine with me up to the bath. After a long soak, I get into my pjs and finish off the pasta. Then the fire gets lit, a movie goes on and I curl up on the sofa with this bowl of heaven that makes me feel right again.

500g (1lb 2oz) linguine or spaghetti
½ tablespoon olive oil
200g (7oz) pancetta lardons or diced streaky bacon
1 garlic clove, crushed
100ml (3½fl oz) double cream or full-fat crème fraîche
2 egg yolks
60g (2¼oz) Parmesan cheese, grated, plus extra to serve
2 tablespoons chopped flat-leaf parsley (optional)
sea salt and freshly ground black pepper

1. Cook the pasta in a large saucepan of salted boiling water for 9 minutes or until the pasta is cooked. Drain, reserving half a cup of the pasta cooking water.

2. While the pasta is cooking, place a frying pan over a medium heat and add the oil. Stir in the pancetta, cook for 2 minutes, then stir in the garlic and cook for a further minute.

3. In a bowl, whisk together the cream or crème fraîche, egg yolks and Parmesan.

4. Reduce the heat under the pancetta to low and stir in the creamy cheese mixture. Season with salt and pepper.

5. Tip the sauce into the cooked pasta along with 1 tablespoon of the reserved pasta cooking water. Add the parsley, if using, and give it all a good stir, adding more pasta cooking water if needed. Scatter over some more grated Parmesan, garnish with another twist of black pepper, serve and smile!

10 Minutes

Speedy Stir It Up

10 MINS / **SERVES 2**

A stir-fry is such a great fast-fix supper. This is one of my favourite ways to stir-fry, with thin slices of juicy beef, fresh crunchy green beans, fragrant basil and zingy chilli all tossed up with oyster and soy sauce. You can swap out the beef for pork, chicken, prawns or tofu. And if you love noodles, use them instead of the rice. You can use any vegetables you have in this recipe – I like to think of it as a great fridge clear-out and I usually make it the evening before I do my food shop.

½ tablespoon oyster sauce

½ tablespoon light soy sauce

½ tablespoon fish sauce

½ tablespoon light soft brown sugar

2 tablespoons vegetable oil

3 garlic cloves, finely chopped

1–2 red chillies, thinly sliced, plus extra to serve

1 sirloin steak, weighing 300g (10½oz), sliced into thin strips

150g (5½oz) green beans, trimmed and halved

a bunch (about 30g/1oz) of Thai basil leaves

250g (9oz) packet of pre-cooked, microwave jasmine rice, cooked according to the packet instructions

1 lime, cut into wedges, to serve

1. In a small bowl, combine the oyster sauce, soy sauce, fish sauce and sugar. Stir to combine.

2. Heat the oil in a large wok over a medium heat until hot. Add the garlic and chillies and stir-fry for 30 seconds or until the garlic starts to turn a light golden colour. Add the steak and green beans and stir-fry over a high heat for 1 minute before adding the bowl of mixed sauces. Cook for a further 3–4 minutes until the beans are al dente and the sauce has reduced by one-third.

3. Add most of the Thai basil, stir through and remove from the heat.

4. Serve on a bed of jasmine rice with lime wedges, a few Thai basil leaves and sliced red chilli on the side.

 If you struggle to find Thai basil, then use half a bunch of Italian basil and half a bunch of roughly chopped tarragon.

Vietnamese Pho

10 MINS / **SERVES 2**

If you haven't made a pho before, you are going to love this! It's so easy to make, fast, delicious and it's like a hug in a bowl. The warming broth, silky noodles, juicy steak, fiery chilli and aromatic spices and herbs are absolutely mouth-watering. You can swap out the beef for chicken or prawns and add spinach, purple sprouting broccoli or frozen peas in there too if you wish.

1 litre (1¾ pints) good-quality beef stock
2cm (¾in) piece of fresh ginger, peeled and grated
1 star anise
½ cinnamon stick
5 cloves
1 teaspoon light soft brown sugar
1 teaspoon light soy sauce
1 teaspoon fish sauce
1 tablespoon vegetable oil
1 thin sirloin steak, weighing about 150g (5½oz)
250g (9oz) fresh rice noodles
10g (¼oz) Thai basil leaves
10g (¼oz) coriander leaves
1 small red chilli, sliced
½ lime, cut into wedges

1. Put the beef stock, ginger, spices, brown sugar, soy sauce and fish sauce in a large saucepan over a medium heat and leave to simmer.

2. Meanwhile, cook the steak by heating the vegetable oil in a frying pan over a high heat until it starts to smoke. Fry the steak for 1 minute on each side before transferring to a plate. (Cook for 2–3 minutes per side if you prefer it well done.)

3. As soon as the steak is cooked, add the noodles to the saucepan of stock and cook according to packet instructions.

4. Once the noodles are cooked, divide between two serving bowls. Thinly slice the steak and arrange on top of the noodles. Scatter over the Thai basil, coriander and chilli and squeeze over a wedge of lime.

Scrambled Eggs Four Ways

10 MINS / **SERVES 2**

Scrambled eggs can be one of the most delicious things – the key is not to over-scramble them; they should be buttery and slightly runny with a light and silky texture. Black or white pepper is a must and whisk the eggs up just before you add them to the pan so that they are lovely and airy. Here are four fantastic ways to transform everyday scrambled eggs into a fabulous supper!

Pancetta & Parmesan Scramble

4 large eggs
1 tablespoon double cream
1 tablespoon butter
100g (3½oz) smoked pancetta lardons
1 garlic clove, crushed
30g (1oz) Parmesan cheese, finely grated
sea salt and freshly ground black pepper

1. Crack the eggs into a bowl, add the double cream and a good twist of black pepper. Whisk well to combine.

2. Melt the butter in a non-stick frying pan over a medium heat. Add the pancetta and fry for 3 minutes until starting to crisp. Add the garlic and fry for 30 seconds. Remove from the pan with a slotted spoon and set aside.

3. Reduce the heat and pour in the beaten eggs. Cook for 2–3 minutes, stirring occasionally, until just cooked but still creamy. Fold in the pancetta and Parmesan. Season to taste.

Green Eggs & Ham

4 large eggs
1 tablespoon full-fat milk
1 tablespoon olive oil
1 small garlic clove, crushed
60g (2¼oz) shredded ham hock
60g (2¼oz) baby spinach, chopped
2 tablespoons finely chopped mixed herbs, such as flat-leaf parsley, dill or basil
sea salt and freshly ground black pepper

1. Crack the eggs into a bowl, add the milk, whisk well and season liberally.

2. Heat the oil in a non-stick frying pan over a medium heat. Add the garlic, ham and spinach and fry until the spinach is just wilted.

3. Reduce the heat and pour in the beaten eggs. Cook for 2–3 minutes, stirring occasionally, until just cooked but still creamy. Fold through the herbs and season to taste.

Kale, Mushroom & Garlic Scramble

4 large eggs

1 tablespoon full-fat milk

1 tablespoon olive oil

125g (4½oz) chestnut mushrooms, sliced

1 tablespoon butter

1 small garlic clove, crushed

75g (2¾oz) kale, shredded

½ tablespoon flat-leaf parsley, roughly chopped

sea salt and freshly ground black pepper

1. Crack the eggs into a bowl, add the milk, whisk well and season liberally.

2. Heat the oil in a non-stick frying pan over a medium heat. Add the mushrooms and fry for 2–3 minutes until golden. Add the butter, garlic and kale and fry for a further minute.

3. Reduce the heat and pour in the beaten eggs. Cook for 2–3 minutes, stirring occasionally, until just cooked but still creamy. Season to taste, scatter over the parsley and serve.

Turkish Scrambled Eggs

1 tablespoon olive oil

½ leek, trimmed, washed and chopped

½ small green pepper, deseeded and finely chopped

1 small garlic clove, crushed

1 large roasted red pepper from a jar, diced

10 cherry tomatoes, quartered

½ teaspoon Aleppo pepper or chilli flakes

½ teaspoon ground cumin

4 large eggs, beaten

½ tablespoon flat-leaf parsley, roughly chopped

sea salt and freshly ground black pepper

1. Heat the oil in a non-stick frying pan over a medium heat. Add the leek, green pepper and garlic and fry for 3 minutes.

2. Add the red pepper, cherry tomatoes, chilli flakes and cumin and cook for a further 2 minutes, squashing the tomatoes with the back of a wooden spoon to break them down a bit.

3. Reduce the heat and pour in the beaten eggs. Cook for 2–3 minutes, stirring occasionally, until just cooked but still creamy. Season to taste, sprinkle over the parsley and serve.

20
Minutes

Vietnamese Summer Rolls with Peanut Dipping Sauce

When we were testing the recipes and photographing this book, this was hands down the favourite recipe in the book! They are simply AMAZING, so promise me you will make them. They will turn your midweek slump into a midweek high. Fresh, crunchy summer rolls dipped in an addictive peanut sauce – heaven!

20 MINS / **SERVES 2**

75g (2¾oz) rice vermicelli noodles
1 teaspoon toasted sesame oil
1 teaspoon light soy sauce
8 x 20cm (8in) summer roll rice paper wrappers
vegetable oil, for greasing
1 large carrot, cut into fine batons (with a julienne peeler)
100g (3½oz) red cabbage, finely shredded
5 spring onions, sliced into batons
½ cucumber, halved, deseeded and sliced into fine batons
60g (2¼oz) roasted salted peanuts, roughly chopped
2 limes, juice of 1 and 1 cut into wedges, to serve
a small handful of mint leaves
a small handful of coriander leaves

For the peanut dipping sauce
100g (3½oz) smooth peanut butter
2 tablespoons light soy sauce
2 teaspoons sriracha
2 tablespoons light soft brown sugar
juice of 1 lime
a pinch of chilli flakes

1. Put the rice noodles in a heatproof bowl and pour over boiling water to just cover. Leave to sit for 2 minutes, then drain and toss with the sesame oil and soy sauce.

2. To make the peanut dipping sauce, place all the ingredients in a bowl. Whisk together to combine and whisk in enough boiling water to make a nice sauce consistency. The amount will depend on the consistency of the peanut butter.

3. Fill a large bowl with warm water. Immerse a rice paper wrapper in the water for 10–15 seconds, drain quickly on a tea towel and transfer to a lightly oiled chopping board.

4. Place a mixture of shredded vegetables, peanuts, noodles and a squeeze of lime juice on the side closest to you. Then place a few mint and coriander leaves on the side furthest from you.

5. Lift the rice paper edge nearest to you and start to roll it up tightly. When you reach halfway, fold the two ends in and keep rolling so the filling is fully enclosed. Place on a plate and cover with a damp tea towel while you make the remaining rolls. Serve with the peanut dipping sauce and wedges of lime.

Try different mixes of shredded, crunchy vegetables. Radishes, beansprouts, lettuce and peppers work really well. If you like, you can also add cooked prawns, tofu sliced into batons or shredded cooked chicken.

20 Minutes

Spiced Falafel Mezze Bowls

20 MINS / **SERVES 2**

I adore this vegetarian bowl of Middle Eastern flavours: couscous brightened up with fresh herbs, zesty lemon and pops of pomegranate to add juiciness and sweetness. The falafels are so easy to make, just pop all the ingredients in a food processor, whizz them up and shape into patties. I love the aromatic spices in the falafel, bringing big flavour to the bowl. Finished off with a drizzle of rich, creamy tahini dressing, this is absolutely delicious!

100g (3½oz) couscous
100ml (3½fl oz) hot vegetable stock
50g (1¾oz) flat-leaf parsley, chopped
50g (1¾oz) mint, chopped
1 medium tomato, diced
2 tablespoons extra virgin olive oil
juice of ½ lemon
a handful of pomegranate seeds
salt and freshly ground black pepper

For the tahini dressing
juice of 1 lemon
1 tablespoon extra virgin olive oil
3 tablespoons tahini
1 small garlic clove, crushed
¾ teaspoon ground cumin

For the falafel
400g (14oz) can of chickpeas, drained, rinsed and patted dry
1 egg, beaten
3 garlic cloves, crushed
½ medium onion, finely chopped
1 tablespoon flat-leaf parsley
1 teaspoon ground cumin
½ teaspoon ground coriander
½ teaspoon fine sea salt
5 heaped tablespoons chickpea (gram) flour
3 tablespoons olive oil

1. First, make the couscous by placing it in a large heatproof bowl and pouring over the hot vegetable stock. Cover the bowl with a plate or clingfilm and leave to stand for 5–6 minutes. Fluff it up with a fork and season to taste.

2. To make the tahini dressing, combine all the ingredients in a bowl and whisk to combine. Season to taste and set aside.

3. Next, make the falafel. In a food processor, combine all the ingredients except the olive oil, and pulse until blended but not smooth – you want some texture. Mould the falafel mix into 10 equal-sized balls, then flatten into patties.

4. Heat the oil in a large non-stick frying pan over a medium heat. Fry the falafel for 3 minutes on side until golden brown and cooked through.

5. Mix together the parsley, mint, tomato, olive oil and lemon juice. Mix through the couscous, season to taste and transfer to bowls. Top with the falafel and a good drizzle of the tahini dressing. Scatter over the pomegranate seeds and serve.

For a quick alternative to falafel, substitute a good dollop of hummus or baba ganoush, or try pan-frying diced aubergine in olive oil, garlic and cumin.

Thai Red Curry with Tofu

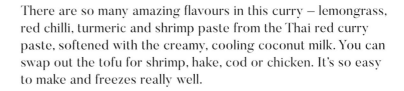

There are so many amazing flavours in this curry – lemongrass, red chilli, turmeric and shrimp paste from the Thai red curry paste, softened with the creamy, cooling coconut milk. You can swap out the tofu for shrimp, hake, cod or chicken. It's so easy to make and freezes really well.

20 MINS / **SERVES 4**

150g (5½oz) jasmine rice, well rinsed in cold running water
2 tablespoons olive oil
1 brown onion, thinly sliced
1 small aubergine, cut into bite-sized chunks
3 garlic cloves, crushed
1 stick of lemongrass, bashed
6 tablespoons Thai red curry paste
1 small courgette, cut into bite-sized chunks
1 red pepper, deseeded and cut into bite-sized chunks
250ml (9fl oz) coconut milk
1 teaspoon caster sugar
100g (3½oz) green beans, trimmed and halved
2 teaspoons fish sauce (optional)
350g (12oz) extra-firm tofu, cut into large cubes
a handful of coriander leaves
1 lime, cut into wedges

1. First, cook the rice. Bring a large saucepan of water to the boil, add the rice and stir. Simmer, uncovered, for 9–10 minutes or until the rice is tender. Drain and set aside.

2. Once the rice is cooking, start the curry. Heat the oil in a heavy-bottomed saucepan or ovenproof casserole dish over a medium heat. Add the onion and aubergine and cook for 2 minutes. Add the garlic, lemongrass and curry paste and fry for 1 minute until fragrant.

3. Add the courgette and red pepper and stir through the coconut milk and sugar. Bring to a simmer and cook for 8 minutes.

4. Add the green beans and continue to cook for a further 5 minutes. Add the fish sauce, if using, and tofu to heat through, then remove from the heat.

5. Serve with the rice, a scattering of coriander leaves and wedges of lime.

This curry is a good base for prawns or meaty fish like cod or salmon (added at the same time as the green beans), or simply leave out the tofu and throw in some more vegetables. Cauliflower, butternut squash, sugar snap peas or Tenderstem broccoli are nice additions.

Indian Spinach & Paneer Curry

20 MINS / **SERVES 4**

Spinach and paneer curry is one of the most loved dishes in India, so yes, it's VERY good! It's made from chunks of a fresh cottage cheese, called paneer, swimming in a lush sauce with fresh spinach. The spinach gives the sauce a naturally thick and creamy consistency. This is one of the milder Indian curries out there, both in heat and spice intensity. The gentle spicing from garam masala, cumin and turmeric plays well with the delicate spinach, without overwhelming it. Meanwhile, the pieces of paneer are like little creamy sponges that absorb all those tasty flavours in the sauce. Plus, it takes just 20 minutes to make – yay!

---

3 tablespoons ghee or vegetable oil

1 large onion, finely chopped

2cm (¾in) piece of fresh ginger, peeled and grated

2 garlic cloves, crushed

1 green chilli, finely chopped

400g (14oz) paneer, cut into 2cm (¾in) cubes

1 teaspoon garam masala

1 teaspoon ground turmeric

1 teaspoon cumin seeds

400g (14oz) spinach, roughly chopped

sea salt and freshly ground black pepper

1. Heat 2 tablespoons of ghee or vegetable oil in a large, heavy-bottomed pan over a medium heat. Add the onion and fry for 5 minutes. Add the ginger, garlic and chilli and continue to fry for a further 5–7 minutes until everything is nicely caramelized. If it starts to look dry, add a little more ghee or oil.

2. While the onion is cooking, heat the remaining ghee or oil in a non-stick frying pan. Add the paneer and fry for 7–8 minutes, turning the cubes regularly until all the sides are golden. Remove to a plate.

3. When the onion is ready, add the spices and fry for 30 seconds, mixing well. Add the spinach to the onion along with 50ml (2fl oz) water. Cook for 2 minutes until wilted.

4. Stir in the paneer and cook for a further 2 minutes until the paneer is heated through. Season to taste and serve with rice or warm naan.

Blanched or roasted cauliflower florets or boiled new potatoes are great vegan alternatives to paneer.

Hasselback Halloumi with Tomatoes, Olives & Capers

Crispy ridged halloumi sat in a bath of salty, olive-y, fiery, aromatic tomato sauce creates such an amazing mouthful! Hasselback-ing the halloumi opens it up so that you get a crispier result. The sauce is so rich and packed with flavour; I use rosemary, but you can swap it out for mint, basil or dried oregano.

20 MINS / **SERVES 2–3**

2 x 250g (9oz) blocks of halloumi
250g (9oz) cherry tomatoes
2 roasted red peppers from a jar, deseeded and roughly chopped
500g (1lb 2oz) mixed olives
1 tablespoon capers
2½ tablespoons extra virgin olive oil
2 garlic cloves, crushed
zest of 1 lemon
1 tablespoon rosemary, finely chopped
½ teaspoon chilli flakes
1 tablespoon flat-leaf parsley, roughly chopped
sea salt and freshly ground black pepper

1. Preheat the oven to 200°C/400°F/gas mark 6.

2. Place a halloumi block between two wooden spoon handles or chopsticks and slice down in 5mm (¼in) intervals. This will leave you with a sliced block that is still attached at the base. Repeat with the second block.

3. Place the halloumi in a small roasting tin. Scatter the tomatoes, peppers, olives and capers around the cheese.

4. In a small bowl, whisk together the olive oil, garlic, lemon zest, rosemary and chilli flakes. Brush this mix over the halloumi and drizzle the rest over the vegetables in the tray. Toss the vegetables to coat evenly. Season with a little salt and lots of pepper. Bake in the oven for 12–15 minutes until the halloumi is golden and the tomatoes have started to blister and burst.

5. Scatter over the parsley and serve with lots of crusty bread.

Paneer would be a good substitute here as it does not melt and turns crispy and golden when roasted. Alternatively, try substituting a block or two of feta (skip stage 2 and leave them whole). The feta will soften and turn deliciously creamy – perfect for dipping bread into.

20 Minutes

Tofu Pad Thai

20 MINS / **SERVES 4**

Pad Thai has definitely become a cult dish on the street-food scene, and there are so many reasons why. It's utterly delicious and satisfying in both flavour and comfort. It's both fresh and vibrant as well as hearty and warming, which makes it a brilliant midweek fast-track supper. This is a variation using tofu, which absorbs all the delicious flavours of spices, herbs and tangy soy and fish sauces, but you can use prawns, chicken or beef if you prefer.

300g (10½oz) dried flat rice noodles

3 tablespoons vegetable oil

a small bunch of spring onions, sliced

2 red chillies, 1 finely chopped, 1 finely sliced to serve

3 garlic cloves, crushed

a small bunch of coriander, stalks finely chopped and leaves picked

1 carrot, peeled and grated

1 courgette, peeled and grated

225g (8oz) Tenderstem broccoli, cut into bite-sized chunks

200g (7oz) smoked tofu, cut into 1cm (½in) cubes

100g (3½oz) roasted salted peanuts, roughly chopped

1 lime, cut into wedges, to serve

For the pad Thai sauce

1 tablespoon fish sauce

3 tablespoons light soft brown sugar

1 tablespoon light soy sauce

1 tablespoon tamarind paste

1 tablespoon sriracha

juice of 1 lime

1. Place the noodles in a large heatproof bowl and pour over boiling water to cover. Leave to soak for 4–5 minutes and rehydrate. Check that the noodles are just softened before draining and running under cold water. Set aside. Be careful not to leave them in the water for too long or they will become too soft.

2. While the noodles are soaking, make the sauce by whisking together all the ingredients to combine.

3. Heat the oil in a large wok and add the spring onions, chopped chilli, garlic and coriander stalks. Fry for 30 seconds until fragrant – be careful that the garlic does not burn.

4. Add the carrot, courgette and broccoli and stir-fry for 2 minutes. Add the noodles, pad Thai sauce and 50ml (2fl oz) water. Stir-fry over a high heat until the water has evaporated, the noodles are cooked and everything is nicely coated in the sauce.

5. Add the tofu and gently toss together until warmed through.

6. Spoon the noodles into bowls, scatter over the peanuts, coriander leaves and sliced chilli. Serve with the lime wedges.

Replace the tofu with small, cooked prawns or shredded, cooked chicken breast if you prefer.

Rocket to the Sky Burger

20 MINS / **SERVES 4**

A guilt-free burger anyone? Crispy halloumi with peppery, zingy rocket pesto, creamy avocado and fresh rocket leaves in a buttery, floury bun, oh yes, this has gotta be good! Fast and fabulous, it's a real crowd-pleaser. I also have lots of alternatives below for the halloumi (if you're not a fan). If you want to bypass making the pesto, then go ahead and buy a good-quality fresh version. You could also add in some roasted peppers for a delicious variation and serve up with roast sweet potato wedges or a green salad.

250g (9oz) block of halloumi, cut into 8 slices
1 tablespoon olive oil
4 brioche buns, halved
30g (1oz) rocket
2 avocados, sliced

For the rocket pesto
30g (1oz) pine nuts, toasted
60g (2¼oz) rocket
1 small garlic clove, crushed
30g (1oz) Parmesan cheese, grated
zest of 1 lemon
130ml (4fl oz) extra virgin olive oil
sea salt and freshly ground black pepper

1. First, make the pesto. Put all the pesto ingredients in a food processor and pulse until well combined, but not totally smooth. Season to taste.

2. Heat a griddle pan over a high heat. Brush the halloumi slices with olive oil and grill for 2 minutes on each side or until nicely charred. Remove from the pan, then place the brioche buns, cut-side down, in the griddle pan to toast for 1 minute.

3. To build the burgers, put a spoonful of pesto on the bottom half of the brioche buns. Top with rocket, sliced avocado, the halloumi and drizzle over more pesto.

For a delicious vegetarian version without the halloumi, thickly slice 4 portobello mushrooms and pan-fry in olive oil with a crushed garlic clove and lots of salt and pepper.

20 Minutes

Turbo Tempeh Tacos

Family taco night in just 20 minutes! These are so fun, easy to whizz up and they look fantastic. I am using a vegan alternative in these tacos called tempeh, which is a plant-based protein that originated in Indonesia. It's made from fermented soybeans that have been formed into a block. Unlike tofu, it has a meaty, firm texture and yummy nutty flavour. Check out the recipe swap below for lots of alternatives to use instead of tempeh.

20 MINS / **SERVES 4**

2 x 200g (7oz) packs of tempeh
1 tablespoon olive oil
1 small brown onion, finely chopped
1 garlic clove, crushed
1 teaspoon smoked paprika
1 teaspoon ground cumin
½ teaspoon chilli flakes
1½ tablespoons light soy sauce
½ tablespoon maple syrup
4 soft corn tortillas, warmed
sea salt and freshly ground black pepper

To serve

½ small red cabbage, thinly sliced
200g (7oz) cherry tomatoes, quartered
2 ripe avocados, mashed with a squeeze of lime juice
a small bunch of coriander, leaves picked
a pinch of chilli flakes
1 lime, sliced into wedges

1. Place the tempeh in a bowl and crumble into small chunks with your hands.

2. Heat the olive oil in a large frying pan over a medium heat. Add the onion and fry for 3 minutes until softened. Add the tempeh and fry for a further 5 minutes until slightly golden.

3. Add the garlic and fry for 30 seconds until fragrant before adding the spices, soy sauce and maple syrup. Stir everything together and fry for a further 2 minutes. Season to taste.

4. Spoon the tempeh mixture into the warm tortillas with the red cabbage, tomatoes and mashed avocado. Top with a scattering of coriander leaves, chilli flakes and a squeeze of lime juice.

Quorn mince, black beans or smoked tofu can be used instead of tempeh to keep it vegan, or if you want a meaty version, try pulled chicken or pork, or minced beef.

Risotto Milanese

20 MINS / **SERVES 2**

This is my favourite recipe in the book, even though I feel guilty saying that as I love all my recipes, but this one... Oh my, oh my, it's a bowl of golden heaven! The first time I ate it was in Milan (where it originates from) in a little garden restaurant during the summer, washed down with a glass of Barbaresco. It's such an incredibly simple recipe – buttery risotto rice swimming in chicken stock peppered with saffron threads – that explodes with colour and flavour. Sometimes the simple things in life are the best things...

25g (1oz) butter

1 tablespoon olive oil

2 shallots, very finely chopped

150g (5½oz) risotto rice, such as arborio or carnaroli

75ml (2½fl oz) dry white wine

a good pinch of saffron threads

500ml (18fl oz) good-quality, hot chicken or vegetable stock

50g (1¾oz) Parmesan cheese, finely grated, plus extra to serve

sea salt and freshly ground black pepper

1. Melt the butter and olive oil in a large saucepan or ovenproof casserole dish over a medium heat. Add the shallots and sauté for 2 minutes. Add the rice and stir for 1 minute until it is coated in the butter.

2. Pour in the wine and add the saffron. Stir to allow the alcohol to evaporate, then slowly add the hot stock, ladle by ladle, stirring constantly until all the stock has been absorbed, the saffron has released its colour and the rice is cooked. This should take about 15 minutes.

3. Stir through the Parmesan and season to taste. Scatter over some more Parmesan to serve.

20 Minutes

Japanese Tempura with Soy Dipping Sauce

One of the most simple and delicious Japanese dishes, tempura is a very light batter that is deep-fried to create a light, crispy coating – you can tempura so many different ingredients, but prawns and vegetables are my favourite. The trick is to make sure that you don't coat the vegetables or prawns too heavily, and the oil should be very hot so that you get that delicious crispiness.

20 MINS / **SERVES 2**

vegetable oil, for deep frying
1 small sweet potato, peeled and cut into 3–4mm (⅛in) slices
4 sprouting broccoli spears
½ small aubergine, cut into 5mm (¼in) slices
6 asparagus spears, woody ends trimmed
6 large king prawns, peeled

For the tempura batter
100g (3½oz) plain flour
100g (3½oz) cornflour
pinch of fine salt
160ml (5½fl oz) ice-cold sparkling water
1 ice cube

For the dipping sauce
2 tablespoons light soy sauce
2 tablespoons mirin
2 tablespoons rice wine vinegar
1cm (½in) piece of fresh ginger, peeled and grated

1. Preheat the oven to 140°C/275°F/gas mark 1.

2. To make the dipping sauce, combine all the ingredients in a small bowl and mix well. Set aside.

3. To make the tempura batter, place the flour, cornflour and salt in a large bowl. Gradually whisk in the sparkling water and add the ice cube.

4. Heat the oil for frying in a large saucepan or deep-fat fryer to 190°C (375°F).

5. Dip the sweet potato slices briefly into the tempura batter, shake off any excess batter and lower carefully into the hot oil. Be careful not to overfill the pan. Fry for 2–3 minutes until light golden. Remove with a slotted spoon and drain briefly on kitchen paper before transferring to a lined baking sheet. Place in the oven to keep warm.

6. Repeat with the remaining vegetables, cooking one type at a time and transferring to the oven to keep warm.

7. Finish by frying the prawns (don't keep these in the oven or they will overcook) and serve immediately with the tempura vegetables and the dipping sauce on the side.

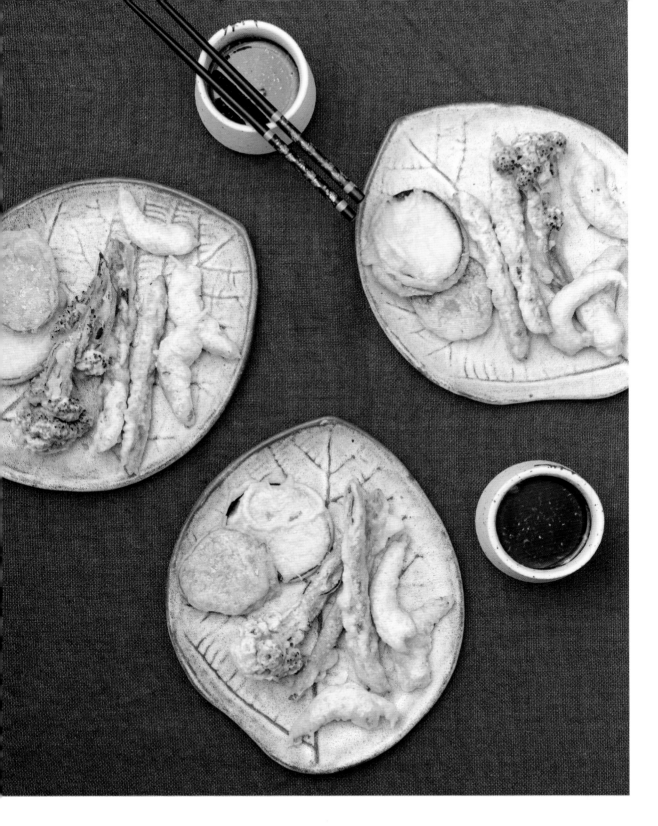

Tuna Poke Bowl

20 MINS / **SERVES 2**

Tuna poke bowl is one of the biggest recent food trends and I totally get why, as it's super healthy, fresh and so delicious! I love the contrast of the textures of the melting tuna against crunchy sesame seeds, dipped into lip-smackingly spicy mayo, followed by a refreshing hit of crunchy vegetables. The key here is not to overcook the fresh tuna – it needs no more than a minute on each side. It should be pink on the inside, if you cook it all the way through, well, it will taste like chicken...

250g (9oz) packet of pre-cooked, microwave brown rice

2 tablespoons light soy sauce

1 teaspoon toasted sesame oil

½ teaspoon sriracha

2 very fresh tuna steaks, weighing about 120g (4¼oz) each

5 tablespoons sesame seeds (black, white or mixed)

1 tablespoon vegetable oil

For the spicy mayonnaise

4 tablespoons mayonnaise

1 tablespoon sriracha

To serve

100g (3½oz) frozen edamame beans

a handful of baby kale or mixed leaf salad

60g (2¼oz) red cabbage, finely shredded

1 carrot, peeled and sliced into thin batons

½ cucumber, halved, deseeded and sliced into thin batons

a handful of radishes, sliced thinly

1 ripe avocado, halved and thinly sliced

2 teaspoons toasted sesame seeds

1 lime, cut into wedges

1. Cook the rice according to the packet instructions, place in two serving bowls and leave to cool.

2. Mix together the soy sauce, sesame oil and sriracha and pour this over the tuna, making sure the marinade coats all sides. Set aside for 10 minutes while you prepare the rest of the recipe.

3. To make the mayonnaise, whisk together the sriracha and mayonnaise along with 1 tablespoon of water.

4. Blanch the edamame beans in salted boiling water for 2–3 minutes.

5. Spread the sesame seeds out on a plate and press each of the tuna steaks into them, coating both sides in seeds.

6. Heat the vegetable oil in a large, non-stick frying pan over a medium heat until very hot. Fry the tuna steaks for 45 seconds per side, so the sesame seeds are golden. This timing sears the outside; if you prefer it more cooked, then increase the cooking time to 1–2 minutes per side.

7. To serve, arrange the vegetables on the bed of rice, slice the tuna and place on top. Drizzle over the spicy mayonnaise, sprinkle over the toasted sesame seeds and serve a wedge of lime on the side.

Substitute very fresh salmon or thick slices of extra-firm tofu for the tuna. These will take on the marinade and coat well in the sesame seeds. You can swap the sriracha sauce for any good hot sauce, such as peri-peri, Jamaican jerk sauce, gochujang or harissa.

Linguine con Vongole

20 MINS / **SERVES 4**

In this dish, sweet, juicy clams go for a lovely swim in white wine, fiery chilli and aromatic garlic to create a fragrant sauce that coats the pasta, which is ridiculously good. You can also make this recipe using fresh mussels, prawns or lobster instead of the traditional clams. It is what is known as a white pasta dish, which means without tomatoes, but you can add good-quality canned or fresh, ripe tomatoes if you wish; I prefer it without. Served up with a cleansing fresh green salad, it's so easy and simple, yet delicious.

2 tablespoons olive oil
2 garlic cloves, crushed
1 red chilli, finely chopped
200ml (7fl oz) white wine
800g (1lb 12oz) fresh clams, cleaned
1 teaspoon dried oregano
500g (1lb 2oz) linguine
2 tablespoons flat-leaf parsley, chopped
sea salt and freshly ground black pepper
lemon wedges, to serve

1. Place a heavy-bottomed saucepan over a medium heat and add the olive oil. Stir in the garlic and chilli and cook for 2 minutes.

2. Add the white wine, clams and dried oregano and increase the heat to high, cover the pan and cook for about 8 minutes until all the clams have opened. (Discard any that have not opened.) Then remove the lid and simmer rapidly for a further 2 minutes to reduce the sauce.

3. Meanwhile, cook the linguine in a large saucepan of salted boiling water. Once the pasta is cooked, drain and set side, keeping back a few tablespoons of the pasta cooking water.

4. Once the clams have all opened, pour the clam sauce into the drained pasta, add the flat-leaf parsley and seasoning and toss so that the sauce coats the pasta. Use the reserved pasta cooking water to loosen the sauce if necessary. Serve straight away with wedges of lemon.

RECIPE SWAP You can swap the fresh chilli with 1 teaspoon of chilli flakes. Spaghetti is a great swap for the linguine.

Seared Tuna Steaks with Wasabi Potato Salad

This is the ultimate fast, no-fuss, but incredibly good supper. The tuna just takes 2 minutes to cook, so make sure you do that at the last minute. The rest is really a case of popping the potatoes in a saucepan and leaving them to cook. The dressing with the added squeeze of wasabi brings it to life! If you want something else alongside, I suggest cooked purple sprouting broccoli or green beans or raw fresh radishes or very thinly sliced fennel.

20 MINS / **SERVES 2**

200g (7oz) Jersey Royal new
  potatoes, scrubbed
100g (3½oz) green beans, trimmed
  and halved
2 tuna steaks, weighing
  about 120g (4¼oz) each
1 tablespoon olive oil
50g (1¾oz) rocket
1 lime, cut into wedges, to serve

For the dressing
3 tablespoons mayonnaise
1 teaspoon wasabi paste
juice of 1 lime
1 tablespoon olive oil
1 garlic clove, crushed
sea salt and freshly ground black
  pepper

1. Bring a pan of salted water to the boil and boil the potatoes for 15 minutes or until tender. Add the green beans to the water for the final 4 minutes of cooking. Drain and set aside.

2. Meanwhile, make the dressing. Whisk together all the ingredients and season to taste.

3. Heat a griddle pan or large non-stick frying pan over a medium heat until hot. Brush the tuna steaks with olive oil, season and cook for 1–2 minutes per side until just seared.

4. Fold the potatoes, rocket and beans together with the dressing. Slice the tuna and serve alongside the vegetables with a wedge of lime for squeezing over.

 A sirloin steak would be a delicious swap for the tuna.

20 Minutes

Crispy Korean Chicken

20 MINS / **SERVES 4**

This one is addictive; I mean it's so good I could have it every week! Sticky, spicy, sweet coating with crunchy sesame seeds. The gochujang (Korean chilli paste) sauce is so simple to make – just mix all the ingredients together in a bowl – it shouldn't take longer than 2 minutes. Then it's just a 5–6-minute dip in hot oil until the chicken is crispy and cooked. I like to serve broccoli and rice or noodles with it – but whatever is easiest for you, any green vegetables would be delicious.

600g (1lb 5oz) skinless chicken thigh fillets, cut into bite-sized chunks
1½ tablespoons toasted sesame oil
½ teaspoon salt
60g (2¼oz) cornflour
4 tablespoons vegetable oil
400g (14oz) Tenderstem broccoli
1 teaspoon light soy sauce
1 tablespoon toasted sesame seeds

For the gochujang sauce
2 tablespoons gochujang (Korean chilli paste)
2 tablespoons tomato ketchup
1 teaspoon caster sugar
1 teaspoon toasted sesame oil
1 teaspoon dark soy sauce
1 teaspoon white wine vinegar
2 teaspoons toasted sesame seeds

1. First make the gochujang sauce by combining all the ingredients and mixing well. Set aside.

2. Put the chicken in a large bowl and add 1 tablespoon of sesame oil and the salt. Mix until the chicken is thoroughly coated. Sprinkle over the cornflour and gently mix until all the chicken is just coated.

3. Heat the vegetable oil in a large frying pan over a medium heat until hot. Add the chicken and spread it out into a single layer. Fry for 2–3 minutes until golden brown before flipping the pieces and cooking for a further 2–3 minutes until crispy and cooked through. Remove from the pan and drain on a few sheets of kitchen paper.

4. Blanch the broccoli in salted boiling water for 2–3 minutes, then remove to a bowl and toss with the remaining sesame oil and the soy sauce.

5. To serve, put the chicken and broccoli on a plate, drizzle over the gochujang sauce and scatter over the sesame seeds.

If you can't find gochujang, then try substituting spicy sriracha sauce.

20 Minutes

Chicken Caesar Salad

20 MINS / **SERVES 2**

Fresh and crunchy romaine lettuce and no-fuss torn croutons, with juicy chicken and a rich, creamy Parmesan dressing – this is so good. You can also make this salad with prawns to bring it closer to a 15-minute supper if you prefer. If you're not a fan of anchovies, then add 2 teaspoons of chopped capers instead so that you still get that salty flavour in the dressing. The dressing will last for a few weeks, so jar and refrigerate any that you have left over.

2½ tablespoons olive oil

1 large, skinless chicken breast

125g (4oz) sourdough bread, torn into bite-sized chunks

1 teaspoon finely chopped rosemary

1 large head romaine lettuce, sliced into 4 wedges

40g (1½oz) Parmesan cheese, shaved into shards using a vegetable peeler

sea salt and freshly ground black pepper

For the Caesar dressing

1 small garlic clove, crushed

3 canned anchovy fillets, finely chopped

½ teaspoon Dijon mustard

2 teaspoons lemon juice

60g (2¼oz) mayonnaise

30ml (1fl oz) extra virgin olive oil

3 tablespoons finely grated Parmesan cheese

1. Preheat the oven to 180°C/350°F/gas mark 4.

2. Heat a griddle pan over a medium heat until hot. Brush the chicken breast with ½ tablespoon of oil, season and place on the griddle. Cook for 8–10 minutes, flipping it halfway through cooking. Check that the chicken is cooked through before removing to a plate and loosely covering with foil.

3. While the chicken is cooking, make the croutons. Place the torn sourdough in a bowl, scatter over the rosemary and a sprinkling of salt and drizzle over 1 tablespoon of olive oil. Toss well so all the bread is coated in the oil. Transfer to a baking tray and bake for 8–10 minutes, turning the croutons a few times, until golden and crispy.

4. Once the chicken is cooked, brush the lettuce wedges with the remaining 1 tablespoon of oil, season and place in the same hot griddle pan. Grill the lettuce on each of the cut sides for 1–2 minutes until nicely marked.

5. Place all the dressing ingredients in a bowl and whisk well to combine. Season to taste.

6. To serve, arrange the lettuce wedges on a serving plate. Slice the chicken and arrange around the lettuce. Sprinkle over the croutons and Parmesan and drizzle over the dressing.

 Crispy bacon lardons would work well, or for a vegetarian version, substitute hard-boiled eggs or vegetarian chicken-style fillets for the chicken, leave the anchovies out of the Caesar dressing and use a vegetarian hard cheese instead of the Parmesan.

Chicken Katsu Ramen

20 MINS / **SERVES 2**

This quick and easy chicken katsu ramen is for those nights when you're craving your favourite bowl of ramen but need it fast and homemade. All cooked in two pans, using healthy, storecupboard ingredients, each bowl is topped with crispy, breaded katsu chicken and simmering underneath is a steaming broth with wholesome kale and comforting noodles.
I love this on a chilly evening, after a long slog of a day, curled up in front of the fire.

1 chicken breast, cut in half lengthways to create 2 flat fillets
25g (1oz) plain flour
2 eggs, beaten
50g (1¾oz) panko breadcrumbs
3 tablespoons vegetable oil
1 litre (1¾ pints) good-quality chicken stock
3 spring onions, sliced
1½ tablespoons light soy sauce
2 x 100g (3½oz) packets of instant ramen noodles
2 handfuls of kale, shredded

1. Dust each chicken fillet in flour, then dip them first into the beaten eggs and then into the panko breadcrumbs to coat.

2. Heat the vegetable oil in a large frying pan over a medium heat and fry the coated chicken fillets for 3–4 minutes on each side or until they are cooked through.

3. Meanwhile, bring the chicken stock to a simmer in a large saucepan and add the spring onions and soy sauce. Add the ramen noodles and cook according to the packet instructions.

4. Add the kale for the final minute of cooking. Transfer the ramen to bowls and top with the chicken katsu cut into slices.

You can swap the kale for Tenderstem broccoli, French beans, cabbage or cavolo nero.

Chicken & Broccoli Salad with Lime Yogurt Dressing

Juicy chicken marinated in zesty lime, aromatic garlic and yogurt that tenderizes the chicken. It only takes 10 minutes to marinate the chicken, so don't skip that part as it makes such a huge difference to the flavour and texture. The crunchy broccoli can be swapped out for roast sweet potato, thinly sliced celery or fennel or grilled courgettes. I know not everyone loves anchovies, so you can leave those out if you prefer and use 1 teaspoon of chopped capers instead. You can swap the chicken for prawns or halloumi, just leave out the yogurt in the marinade. Sesame or sunflower seeds are a good alternative to the pumpkin seeds.

20 MINS / **SERVES 2**

zest and juice of 1 lime
200g (7oz) natural yogurt
2 garlic cloves, crushed
2 skinless chicken breasts
2 anchovy fillets
1 tablespoon basil leaves
1 tablespoon mint leaves
175g (6oz) broccoli, cut into small florets
1 head romaine lettuce, split into leaves
1 ripe avocado, sliced
2 teaspoons pumpkin seeds
sea salt and freshly ground black pepper

1. In a bowl, mix together half the lime zest and juice with half the yogurt and garlic. Season with salt and pepper.

2. Flatten the chicken between two sheets of clingfilm using a rolling pin to flatten to about 1cm (½in) thick. Place the flattened chicken in the yogurt marinade, making sure the chicken is completely coated. Leave to marinate for 10 minutes in the fridge.

3. To make the dressing, place the remaining yogurt, garlic, lime zest and juice, anchovies, basil and mint in a blender and whizz until smooth.

4. Cook the broccoli in a pan of boiling water for 3 minutes, drain and set aside to cool.

5. Place a frying pan over a medium–high heat and cook the marinated chicken for 5 minutes on each side.

6. Arrange the lettuce leaves, broccoli and avocado on two plates (or a sharing platter) and top with the sliced cooked chicken. Drizzle the dressing over the salad and sprinkle the pumpkin seeds on top.

Nasi Goreng

20 MINS / **SERVES 4**

The literal translation of Nasi Goreng is 'fried rice' in Indonesian and Malay. The thing that distinguishes it from other fried rice dishes is the sauce, which is made with kecap manis, a sweet soy sauce that stains the rice dark brown and caramelizes the rice as it cooks – and is now available in most supermarkets. I love the unique dark brown, caramelized colour of the rice. It is such a simple recipe, and it's one of my favourite Indonesian foods. I am using chicken but you can use prawns (most traditionally used), or tofu for a vegan alternative.

4 tablespoons vegetable oil

2 skinless chicken breasts, cut into small chunks

1 red bird's eye chilli, finely chopped

7 spring onions, thinly sliced

1cm (½in) piece of fresh ginger, peeled and crushed

3 large garlic cloves, crushed

150g (5½oz) spring greens, shredded

2 x 250g (9oz) packets of pre-cooked, microwave long-grain rice

½ tablespoon tomato purée

½ tablespoon tomato ketchup

1 tablespoon kecap manis (Indonesian sweet soy sauce, available in most supermarkets)

1 tablespoon light soy sauce

4 large eggs

2 tablespoons coriander, chopped

sea salt

1. Heat 1 tablespoon of oil in a large wok over a medium heat. Add the chicken and stir-fry for 3–4 minutes until nicely golden and cooked through. Remove with a slotted spoon and set aside.

2. Add 2 tablespoons of oil to the wok. Add the chilli and spring onions and stir-fry for 30 seconds, then add the ginger and garlic. Stir-fry for 30 seconds until aromatic, being careful to not let them burn. Throw in the spring greens and cook for 2 minutes until they start to wilt.

3. Add the rice, tomato purée, ketchup, kecap manis, soy sauce and 3 tablespoons of water. Stir-fry for 3–4 minutes, making sure to break up any clumps of rice and to coat everything well in the sauce.

4. Add the chicken back to the wok and cook for a minute until the chicken is warmed through.

5. In a separate frying pan, add the remaining tablespoon of oil and fry the eggs for 4–5 minutes. Season with salt.

6. Spoon the fried rice into bowls, top with a fried egg and shower over the coriander.

RECIPE SWAP Prawns, halloumi and tofu are good swaps for the chicken. Soy sauce can replace the kecap manis if you are finding it difficult to get.

20 Minutes

Moroccan Spiced Lamb

Lamb chops or cutlets are such a brilliant quick-fix supper as they only take about 8 minutes to cook and really hit the spot! I love spicing them up with this yogurt marinade. It does two things – packs the lamb with flavour and also tenderizes the meat, so this is definitely a step not to be skipped. If you don't have any yogurt just leave it out, and if you don't have harissa just use a teaspoon of smoked paprika instead.

20 MINS / **SERVES 2**

4–6 lamb chops, depending on size
1 tablespoon olive oil

For the yogurt marinade
100g (3½oz) natural yogurt
1 tablespoons olive oil
1 tablespoon harissa paste
1 garlic clove, crushed
1 teaspoon ground cumin

For the bulgur wheat
240ml (8½fl oz) chicken stock
120g (4¼oz) bulgur wheat
150g (5½oz) green beans, trimmed and halved
2 tablespoons extra virgin olive oil
juice of 1 lemon
a handful of flat-leaf parsley, roughly chopped
a handful of mint leaves, roughly chopped
2 tablespoons pine nuts
a handful of pomegranate seeds
sea salt and freshly ground black pepper

1. In a large bowl, mix together the marinade ingredients along with a liberal sprinkling of salt and pepper. Add the lamb chops and coat well on all sides with the marinade. Set aside for 5 minutes.

2. In a large saucepan, heat the stock and add the bulgur wheat. Simmer, covered, for 10–15 minutes until most of the water has been absorbed. Remove from the heat, drain off any excess liquid and set aside.

3. While the bulgur wheat is cooking, bring a separate large saucepan of salted water to the boil and blanch the green beans for 3–4 minutes until just tender. Drain and plunge into cold water to stop them cooking.

4. Meanwhile, heat the oil in a large frying pan over a high heat. Lift the lamb chops out of the marinade bowl and cook for 4 minutes on each side. Remove to a plate and cover loosely with foil to rest for 5 minutes.

5. Fluff up the bulgur wheat with a fork before mixing in the green beans and remaining bulgur wheat ingredients. Season to taste and serve alongside the lamb chops.

 You can use couscous as a swap for the bulgur wheat. The lamb chops can also be replaced with pork chops or chicken.

Happy Hotdogs with Oh Yeah Yum Slaw

Don't they make you a smidge happier just looking at them?! They are so fun to serve up for a relaxed supper. Grill the hot dogs up on the barbecue if it's sunny outside. It's definitely worth going the extra mile and buying brioche buns (they freeze really well too) for the soft, buttery texture. The Oh Yeah Yum Slaw is fantastic with tons of things – burgers, grilled chicken, steak, or lamp chops.

20 MINS   **SERVES 4**

1 tablespoon olive oil
8 good-quality spicy sausages
8 brioche hot dog buns

For the oh yeah yum slaw
100g (3½oz) mayonnaise
50g (1¾oz) full-fat crème fraîche
2 tablespoons flat-leaf parsley, finely chopped
½ green cabbage, peeled and cut into strips
2 celery sticks, thinly sliced
2 carrots, peeled and grated
juice of 1 lemon
sea salt and freshly ground black pepper
mustard and tomato ketchup, to serve

1. Preheat the oven to 140°C/275°F/gas mark 1.

2. Place a frying pan over a medium heat and add the oil. Cook the sausages in the pan for 10 minutes (or until cooked), turning every few minutes.

3. While the sausages are cooking, make the oh yeah yum slaw. Toss all the ingredients together in a large serving bowl and season with salt and pepper.

4. Warm the hot dog buns in the oven for a few minutes. Pop the cooked spicy sausages in the buns, followed by a generous spoonful of the oh yeah yum slaw and some mustard and tomato ketchup.

20 Minutes

Crispy Chilli Beef Noodles

Crispy, sweet, spicy and lip-lickingly good! The trick with this dish is to slice the steak as thinly as you can and cook it in a hot frying pan. Do it in batches – that way it crisps up rather than stews. You can swap out the beef for chicken, pork, prawns or tofu.

20 MINS / **SERVES 2**

2 nests of dried egg noodles

2½ tablespoons toasted sesame oil, plus extra for the noodles

1 tablespoon light soy sauce, plus extra for the noodles

2 thin-cut beef steaks, weighing about 125g (4½oz) each, cut into thin strips

1 egg, beaten

100g (3½oz) cornflour

vegetable oil, for deep-frying

1 garlic clove, crushed

1cm (½in) piece of fresh ginger, peeled and grated

1 small red chilli, finely chopped

1 carrot, cut into long, thin strips with a julienne peeler

1 small red pepper, cut into thin strips

For the sauce

1 tablespoon dark soy sauce

2 tablespoons light soy sauce

6 tablespoons rice wine vinegar

2 tablespoons tomato ketchup

2 tablespoons sweet chilli sauce

2 tablespoons honey

1. Bring a large pan of water to the boil and simmer the noodles for 4 minutes or cook according to the packet instructions. Drain and drizzle over a splash of sesame oil and soy sauce and set aside somewhere warm.

2. While the noodles are cooking, mix together the sauce ingredients.

3. In a separate bowl, combine the beef, ½ tablespoon of sesame oil, the soy sauce and beaten egg. Mix really well to coat the beef fully.

4. Place the cornflour in a large bowl, add the beef and toss until coated. At first it will clump together, but as the egg coating absorbs the cornflour the pieces should separate.

5. Half-fill a pan with vegetable oil or heat a deep-fat fryer to 180°C (350°F). Fry the beef in two batches for 5 minutes until golden brown and crispy. Remove and drain on kitchen paper.

6. Heat the remaining 2 tablespoons of sesame oil in a large wok over a high heat. Add the garlic, ginger and chilli and stir-fry for 30 seconds until fragrant. Add the carrot and red pepper and stir-fry for 4–5 minutes or until they start to soften. Pour in the sauce and bring to the boil. Add the crispy beef back to the pan briefly just to coat well in the sauce.

7. Spoon the beef and sauce over the noodles and serve.

Steak with Thai Sriracha Sauce

20 MINS / **SERVES 2**

OK, let's chat a little about steak first... When shopping for your steak, you want a steak that's been aged for at least 28 days. It should be a dull, dark, not bright, red. The darker the colour usually means it's been aged for longer and will therefore be more tender. The next thing is the marbling. A great steak will have lots of thin threads of fat running through it – this is what's known as marbling, and it's where all the flavour comes from. If you can't get your hands on a well-aged steak, then here's what I do: I suspend the steak in a sieve sitting over a bowl in the fridge for a couple of days – this helps improve the tenderness.

2 sirloin steaks, weighing about 140g (5oz) each
olive oil, for frying
sea salt and freshly ground black pepper

For the sauce
½ green pepper, deseeded and roughly chopped
1 lemongrass stalk, outer layers discarded and finely sliced
2–3 green chillies, roughly chopped
15g (½oz) coriander
15g (½oz) mint
20g (¾oz) Thai basil
15g (½oz) chives
10g (¼) solid creamed coconut, crumbled or grated
2 garlic cloves, crushed
1cm (½in) piece of fresh ginger, peeled and grated
½ teaspoon ground turmeric
juice of 2 limes
50ml (2fl oz) vegetable oil

1. Remove the steaks from the fridge and put on a plate. If you're not pressed for time, try to do this at least 30 minutes before you cook them so that the meat comes up to room temperature – it will result in a more tender meat.

2. To make the Thai sriracha sauce, place the green pepper, lemongrass and chillies in a food processor and pulse until finely chopped. Add all the herbs, creamed coconut, garlic, ginger and turmeric and pulse until everything is chopped. Add the lime juice and vegetable oil and pulse until it reaches a pesto-like consistency. Season with salt to taste.

3. Heat a griddle or frying pan over a high heat until smoking hot. Lightly brush the steak with a little olive oil and season with salt and pepper. Place the prepared steaks on the hot pan, and cook to the following times:

   • **Medium-rare: 2 minutes on each side**
   • **Medium: 2½ minutes on each side**
   • **Medium-well done: 3 minutes on each side**

4. Let the steaks rest for about 3 minutes before serving, to allow the juices that have been drawn to the surface to relax back into the meat. Slice the steak and serve drizzled with the Thai sriracha sauce.

30
Minutes

The Ultimate Mac & Cheese

30 MINS / **SERVES 4**

I have so many variations on this favourite comfort food that I feel I could write a whole book on it! However, this recipe really is the ultimate: it's very creamy (which is essential in a mac and cheese), and the topping is lovely and crunchy (also essential), thanks to the panko breadcrumbs. You can add chopped almonds, pecans or hazelnuts into the topping too. Also, you can mix blue cheese, crispy pancetta, chorizo or truffle oil into the cheese mixture. Serve with a refreshing green-leaf salad to balance the cheese takeover!

280g (10oz) macaroni
700ml (1¼ pints) full-fat milk
1 bay leaf
40g (1½oz) butter
1 garlic clove, crushed
3 tablespoons plain flour
170g (6oz) mature Cheddar cheese, grated
60g (2¼oz) Gruyère cheese, grated
20g (¾oz) Parmesan cheese, grated
1 teaspoon Dijon mustard
a dash of Worcestershire sauce
a grating of fresh nutmeg
sea salt and freshly ground black pepper

For the topping
4 heaped tablespoons panko breadcrumbs
1 tablespoon finely grated Parmesan cheese
a pinch of smoked paprika

1. Bring a large pan of salted water to the boil and cook the macaroni according to packet instructions. Drain and set aside. While the pasta is cooking, make the sauce.

2. Pour the milk into a saucepan and add the bay leaf. Heat over a medium heat until hot, but not boiling.

3. Once the milk is hot, melt the butter in a separate large, heavy-based saucepan, add the garlic and gently fry for 30 seconds or until aromatic and just starting to turn golden. Stir in the flour and cook for 1 minute. Slowly whisk in the hot milk a little at a time until it is all combined and the sauce is smooth. Bring the mixture up to a simmer and cook for 5 minutes before stirring in the cheeses, mustard, Worcestershire sauce and nutmeg and season to taste. Whisk to make sure the cheeses have all melted and combined with the sauce. Remove the bay leaf.

4. Fold the cooked macaroni through the sauce and transfer to an ovenproof dish. Scatter over the breadcrumbs, Parmesan and paprika.

5. Place the dish under a hot grill for 2–3 minutes until the topping is crunchy and golden.

Nut Roast Balls, Onion Gravy & Greens

This hearty nut roast is jam-packed with all the good stuff, and the onion gravy is full of flavour. It's a fantastic vegan alternative to a roast dinner, and even though I'm not vegan, I love this dish – the nutty flavours of the roast balls are so good. You might question the peanut butter addition, but it adds a delicious nutty richness to the overall taste. The gravy is so good you will want to use it to go with all your roasts – the dark soy sauce, rosemary and garlic add so much to the flavour.

30 MINS   **SERVES 2**

150g (5½oz) mixed nuts, such as
  peanuts, almonds and hazelnuts
2 tablespoons olive oil
½ small red onion, finely chopped
1 garlic clove, crushed
1 celery stick, chopped
1 small carrot, peeled and grated
75g (2¾oz) chestnut mushrooms,
  finely chopped or grated
1 teaspoon thyme leaves
50g (1¾oz) ground almonds
50g (1¾oz) panko breadcrumbs
1 tablespoon smooth peanut butter
3 tablespoons chickpea (gram) flour
6 tablespoons vegetable oil
150g (5½oz) leafy greens, such as
  spring greens, kale or cavolo nero
a drizzle of extra virgin olive oil
sea salt and freshly ground black
  pepper

For the onion gravy
2 tablespoons olive oil
1 medium onion, very finely sliced
1 small garlic clove, crushed
1 tablespoon plain flour
250ml (9fl oz) hot vegetable stock
1½ teaspoons dark soy sauce
1 teaspoon yeast extract
1 sprig of rosemary

1. Preheat the oven to 180°C/350°F/gas mark 4.

2. Start the gravy first. In a medium saucepan, heat the oil over a medium heat and add the onion and garlic. Sauté for 10-12 minutes until deeply caramelized.

3. Meanwhile, make the nut roast balls. Place the mixed nuts in a heatproof bowl and pour over enough boiling water to cover. Leave for 2 minutes before draining.

4. While the nuts are soaking, heat the olive oil in a large frying pan over a medium heat. Add the red onion, garlic, celery, carrot, mushrooms and thyme. Fry for 5 minutes until everything has softened and the onion and mushrooms have caramelized a little.

5. Add the drained nuts to the pan. Stir together and season well before transferring to a food processor. Add the ground almonds, breadcrumbs, peanut butter, chickpea flour and some seasoning and pulse until combined; you still want the nuts to have some texture, but the mix should be a bit sticky and well combined. Divide the mixture into 10 balls.

6. Heat the vegetable oil in a large non-stick frying pan over a medium heat. Add the balls and fry for 5 minutes, moving them around so they turn golden brown all over. Transfer to a lined baking tray and roast in the oven for 10 minutes.

30 Minutes

7. While the nut roast balls are in the oven, finish the gravy and steam the greens. To finish the gravy, stir the flour through the caramelized onions in the pan and cook for 2 minutes until the flour smells nutty. Pour over the hot vegetable stock and stir through the soy sauce and yeast extract and add the rosemary sprig. Bring to the boil, then reduce the heat and simmer for 5 minutes or until the gravy reaches a nice consistency. Remove the rosemary sprig before serving.

8. Place the leafy greens in a steamer and cook for 3–5 minutes until tender. Drizzle over some extra virgin olive oil and sprinkle with salt. Serve the nut roast balls on a bed of greens and pour over the onion gravy.

You can swap the soy sauce and yeast extract in the gravy with a glass of red wine. Cabbage is a great swap for cavolo nero or kale.

Cherry Tomato, Asparagus & Herbed Ricotta Tart

I love ready-made puff pastry sheets – my freezer is stacked with them. A lot of chefs can be a bit snooty about them, but I am definitely not. They are brilliant; roll them out, cover them with delicious toppings and pop them in the oven, and you've got a delicious supper. I love to do a tart a week using different vegetables that I'm growing in the garden. The whipped ricotta with herbs, Parmesan and garlic is sensational and should be added to all your vegetable tarts. If you have some delicious homemade pesto (or a good shop-bought one), then drizzle it over the tart for an extra layer of flavour.

30 MINS / **SERVES 6**

320g (11½oz) ready-rolled puff
   pastry sheet
300g (10½oz) ricotta
1 garlic clove, crushed
50g (1¾oz) Parmesan cheese,
   finely grated
1 tablespoon basil, finely chopped
2 tablespoons chives, finely
   chopped
1 tablespoon flat-leaf parsley,
   finely chopped
zest of 1 lemon
200g (7oz) asparagus spears,
   woody ends trimmed
300g (10½oz) cherry tomatoes,
   halved
1 tablespoon olive oil
1 egg, beaten
sea salt and freshly ground black
   pepper

1. Preheat the oven to 200°C/400°F/gas mark 6. Unroll the puff pastry onto a lined baking sheet.

2. Using a sharp knife, score a 2cm (¾in) border around the edge of the pastry, being careful to not cut all the way through. Prick the pastry inside the border all over with a fork. This will help to stop it puffing up in the oven.

3. In a medium bowl, whisk together the ricotta, garlic, Parmesan, chopped herbs and lemon zest and season liberally. Spread the ricotta mix over the tart inside the border. Place the asparagus spears over the tart and dot around the cherry tomatoes, cut-side up. Press them down gently so that they sink slightly into the ricotta mix and brush lightly with olive oil.

4. Brush the pastry border with the beaten egg and bake for 20 minutes until the pastry is golden and cooked through. Season with pepper and serve.

 Roast pumpkin, butternut squash, Tenderstem broccoli and courgettes are good swaps for the tomatoes and asparagus. Goat's cheese is a great alternative to the ricotta.

30 Minutes

Sweet Potato, Feta & Caramelized Red Onion Frittata

Heavenly caramel-like sweet potatoes with creamy feta and sweetened red onions – this frittata is epic in flavour! So simple to make with really easy-to-buy ingredients, yep, it's a stress-free night of deliciousness. You can use goat's cheese or ricotta instead of the feta if you wish. Serve the frittata hot, warm or cold and a slice is fantastic the next day, too. One word of advice: don't overcook the frittata otherwise it will be dry and lacking in flavour.

30 MINS / **SERVES 4**

300g (10½oz) sweet potato, peeled and cut into 1cm (½in) cubes
1 tablespoon butter
1 tablespoon olive oil
2 red onions, very thinly sliced
1 garlic clove
1 teaspoon thyme leaves, plus small sprigs to serve
1 tablespoon balsamic vinegar
1 tablespoon flat-leaf parsley, chopped, plus extra to serve
6 large eggs, beaten and liberally seasoned
125g (4½oz) feta cheese
sea salt

1. Bring a large saucepan of salted water to the boil and cook the sweet potato for 8–10 minutes or until tender. Drain well.

2. While the potato is cooking, heat the butter and olive oil in a large, ovenproof frying pan over a medium heat and add the red onions. Fry the onions for 8 minutes until nicely caramelized and soft. Add the garlic, thyme and balsamic vinegar and fry for a further 2 minutes until the garlic is fragrant and the vinegar has evaporated.

3. Stir the parsley through the onions, then scatter the sweet potatoes around the pan.

4. Pour over the beaten egg and swirl it around to fully cover the base of the pan. Break the feta into chunks and scatter over the egg. Cook over a low heat for 5–6 minutes until the sides and the underside of the frittata are starting to look set.

5. Transfer to a hot grill for 3–4 minutes or until the top of the frittata is golden and it is set all the way through. Scatter over some thyme and parsley to serve.

 Roast butternut squash or pumpkin are great swaps for the sweet potato. Goat's cheese or ricotta would be equally as delicious as the feta.

Spinach, Leek & Feta Filo Pastry Tart

30 MINS / **SERVES 4**

This was one of the most watched recipe videos on my Instagram. It looks amazing, it's so easy to make as I use shop-bought filo pastry (stock up on that), and it tastes SO good! Creamy, crunchy, buttery, caramel flavours and textures with fresh green vegetables mingled through the tart. You can make this a day ahead if you need to, then just warm it through in the oven. Serve with a lovely, fresh green salad.

2 tablespoons olive oil

2 leeks, trimmed, washed and sliced

2 garlic cloves, crushed

200g (7oz) spinach

2 eggs

200ml (7fl oz) double cream

80g (2¾oz) Parmesan cheese, grated

a grating of fresh nutmeg

50g (1¾oz) butter, melted

4 sheets of filo pastry

100g (3½oz) crumbled feta cheese or ricotta

sea salt and freshly ground black pepper

1. Preheat the oven to 190°C/375°F/gas mark 5.

2. Place a saucepan over a low heat and add the oil, then stir in the leeks and garlic. Cover and cook for 4 minutes. Remove the lid and stir in the spinach. Cook for a further 1 minute, then remove from the heat and allow to cool a little.

3. While the leeks are cooking, in a large mixing bowl, whisk the eggs and then pour in the cream and grated Parmesan. Season with salt, pepper and a grating of fresh nutmeg and whisk again. Fold in the cooked leeks and spinach.

4. Grease a 23cm (9in) loose-bottomed tart tin with some of the melted butter. Brush each sheet of filo pastry with melted butter and place the filo pastry sheets in the tin, one by one, at different angles so that each corner of the sheet isn't overlapping on the rim. Gently scrunch the pastry to form a pretty rim. Spoon the tart filling into the centre of the tin and using the back of the spoon spread the mixture out evenly. Crumble over the feta and gently press it into the mix.

5. Bake for 8 minutes, then cover the edges of the tart loosely with foil to stop the filo getting too dark and bake for a further 12–15 minutes or until the centre is just set.

You can swap the spinach for kale, cabbage, cavolo nero or blanched asparagus spears. Goat's cheese or ricotta are good swaps for the feta.

Singaporean Black Pepper Prawns

Fast, fiery and juicy prawns along with rice and pak choi to make a more substantial supper. If you use pre-cooked, microwave rice, then this dish will take just 10 minutes to make.

30 MINS / **SERVES 2**

150g (5½oz) basmati rice, washed well

1 tablespoon olive oil

1 tablespoon butter

1 small red chilli, deseeded and chopped

1cm (½in) piece of fresh ginger, peeled and chopped

2 garlic cloves, crushed

1 teaspoon black peppercorns, coarsely ground

2 pak choi, sliced

1 teaspoon oyster sauce

1 teaspoon light soy sauce

1 teaspoon dark soy sauce

1 teaspoon caster sugar

250g (9oz) jumbo king prawns, peeled

4 spring onions, finely sliced, plus extra to serve

sea salt

1. Start by cooking the rice. Add it to a large pan of salted boiling water and cook for 10–12 minutes, or until tender. Once cooked, drain, rinse with boiling water and set aside.

2. Once the rice is cooked, start the prawns. In a large wok, heat the oil and butter over a high heat. Add the chilli, ginger, garlic and pepper. Sauté for 1–2 minutes until the pepper is fragrant and the garlic is starting to turn golden.

3. Add the pak choi and stir-fry for 2-3 minutes until it has wilted. Add the oyster sauce, both soy sauces, caster sugar and 1 tablespoon of water, followed by the prawns and spring onions. Stir-fry over a high heat for 5 minutes until the prawns have just turned pink and are well coated in sauce and pepper. Taste for seasoning, adding a splash more soy if it needs it.

4. Serve immediately on a bed of rice with a scattering of sliced spring onion.

For a healthier alternative, swap the white basmati rice to brown basmati. You can swap the fresh chilli to ½ teaspoon of chilli flakes.

Creamy Smoked Trout, Pea & Mint Spaghetti

The smoky fish swimming in the cream, and the added flavours of lemon, mint, sweet peas and the silky leeks are so delicious! The asparagus spears add flavour and crunchy texture, just make sure not to overcook them. If anything, undercook them so you keep that crunch.

30 MINS / **SERVES 4**

1 tablespoon olive oil

1 leek, trimmed, washed and thinly sliced

12 asparagus spears, woody ends trimmed, cut into 5cm (2in) lengths

120g (4¼oz) frozen peas

120ml (4fl oz) double cream

175g (6oz) hot-smoked trout, skin removed and flaked

zest and juice of 1 lemon

500g (1lb 2oz) spaghetti

1 tablespoon mint leaves, chopped

sea salt and freshly ground black pepper

1. Heat the oil in a frying pan over a low heat. Stir in the leek and cook, stirring, for 10 minutes, or until soft. Next, add the asparagus and peas, and cook, stirring, for 3 minutes. Pour in the cream, then add the smoked trout, lemon zest and juice. Stir and cook for 2 minutes. Season with salt and pepper.

2. Meanwhile, cook the spaghetti in a large saucepan of salted boiling water according to the packet instructions. Once the pasta is cooked, drain and set side, reserving a few tablespoons of the pasta cooking water, which you can use to stop the pasta from sticking together.

3. Add the pasta, reserved pasta cooking water and mint to the smoked trout mixture and stir until well combined. Serve.

You can swap the smoked trout with hot-smoked salmon.

30 Minutes

Four Ways with Cod

30 MINS / SERVES 4

I've called this 'four ways with cod', but you could use any of these sauces with other meaty fish like hake, haddock, halibut, ling or salmon. They are such easy ways to prepare a healthy, fast supper, just add some vegetables and rice or a baked potato and you're sorted!

Cod with Saffron Aioli

4 cod fillets, skin on, weighing about 150g (5½oz) each
a pinch of saffron threads
1 tablespoon boiling water
3 egg yolks
1 teaspoon Dijon mustard
1 garlic clove, crushed
1 tablespoon white wine vinegar
100ml (3½fl oz) vegetable oil
100ml (3½fl oz) extra virgin olive oil
sea salt and freshly ground black pepper

1. Preheat the oven to 180°C/350°F/gas mark 4. Place the fish on a baking tray and season with salt and pepper. Roast for 20 minutes.

2. Place the saffron in a small bowl and add the boiling water. Leave for 10 minutes to infuse and cool.

3. In a large bowl, combine the egg yolks, Dijon mustard, garlic and white wine vinegar. Whisk well to combine. Slowly whisk the vegetable oil and olive oil into the egg mixture to form a thick mayonnaise. Once all the oil has been added, whisk in the saffron and water. Season to taste. Serve the cod topped with the saffron aioli.

Cod with Black Olive Tapenade

4 cod fillets, skin on, weighing about 150g (5½oz) each
200g (7oz) good-quality pitted black olives in oil, drained
1 garlic clove
2 anchovy fillets
1 tablespoon capers
75ml (2½fl oz) extra virgin olive oil
zest of ½ lemon, plus 1 tablespoon juice
sea salt and freshly ground black pepper

1. Preheat the oven to 180°C/350°F/gas mark 4. Place fish on a baking tray and season with salt and pepper. Roast for 20 minutes.

2. Place the olives, garlic, anchovies, capers, oil and lemon zest and juice in a small food processor and pulse to form a very chunky paste. Season to taste.

3. Serve the cod topped with the tapenade.

Cod with Gremolata Crust

2 large garlic cloves, crushed

15g (½oz) flat-leaf parsley,
 finely chopped

zest of 1 lemon

60g (2¼oz) panko breadcrumbs

1 tablespoon olive oil, plus extra for
 drizzling

4 cod fillets, skin on, weighing
 about 150g (5½oz) each

sea salt and freshly ground black
 pepper

1. Preheat the oven to 180°C/350°F/gas mark 4.

2. In a small bowl, combine the garlic, parsley, lemon zest, breadcrumbs and oil and mix really well to evenly distribute the garlic and parsley. Add a pinch of salt and a liberal amount of pepper.

3. Place the cod on a baking tray, season and divide the gremolata between the pieces of fish, pressing it down to form a crust. Drizzle with olive oil and bake for 20 minutes until the cod is cooked and the gremolata is golden.

Cod with Romesco Sauce

4 cod fillets, skin on, weighing
 about 150g (5½oz) each

125g (4½oz) whole blanched
 almonds

250g (9oz) roasted red peppers
 from a jar, drained, deseeded
 and roughly chopped

1 garlic clove, crushed

1 tablespoon red wine vinegar

1 teaspoon smoked paprika

75ml (2½fl oz) extra virgin olive oil

sea salt and freshly ground black
 pepper

1. Preheat the oven to 180°C/350°F/gas mark 4. Place the fish on a baking tray and season with salt and pepper. Roast for 20 minutes.

2. Heat a large frying pan over a medium heat and add the almonds. Dry toast for 3–4 minutes until they are nicely toasted.

3. Place the almonds, peppers, garlic, red wine vinegar and smoked paprika in a food processor and pulse until combined but still a little chunky. Leave the food processor running and gradually drizzle in the olive oil to make a thick sauce. Don't blend until totally smooth as some texture works well here. Season to taste.

4. Serve the cod topped with the romesco sauce.

Goan Fish Curry

30 MINS / **SERVES 4**

From the beautiful paradise of Goa comes this amazing curry with a deeply aromatic tomato and coconut sauce, peppered with delicious Indian spices, and prawns and haddock gently poaching away while they absorb all the flavours. You can use so many different varieties of fish in this recipe – hake, ling, whiting, cod or even shrimps. Don't cook the fish for longer than 5 minutes, that's really all it needs, and it will become dry if it overcooks.

300g (10½oz) basmati rice, washed well
2 tablespoons vegetable oil
1 brown onion, finely chopped
2 green chillies, deseeded and finely chopped
3 garlic cloves, roughly chopped
3cm (1¼in) piece of fresh ginger, peeled and grated
1 teaspoon mustard seeds
½ teaspoon ground cloves
1 teaspoon ground cumin
2 teaspoons ground coriander
1 teaspoon ground turmeric
1 teaspoon garam masala
1 bay leaf
1 large tomato, roughly chopped
400ml (14fl oz) coconut milk
350g (12oz) haddock, cut into 2.5cm (1in) chunks
250g (9oz) king prawns, peeled
150g (5½oz) sugar snap peas
2 tablespoons coriander leaves, roughly chopped
sea salt and freshly ground black pepper

1. Start by cooking the rice. Add it to a large pan of salted boiling water and cook for 10-12 minutes, or until tender. Once cooked, drain, then rinse with boiling water and set aside.

2. While the rice is cooking, heat the oil in a large, ovenproof casserole dish or saucepan. Add the onion and fry for 10 minutes until softened and golden.

3. Add the chillies, garlic, ginger, all the spices and the bay leaf. Fry for 2 minutes, stirring constantly, until aromatic. Add the chopped tomato and fry for 2 minutes.

4. Pour in the coconut milk, add a pinch of salt and some pepper and bring to a simmer. Simmer for 8–10 minutes until the sauce has thickened nicely.

5. Gently stir through the haddock, prawns and sugar snap peas. Simmer for a further 5 minutes, check the seasoning and serve with the cooked rice and a scattering of coriander leaves.

You can swap the sugar snaps for French beans, peas, or broccoli heads.

Fish & Chips with Zippy Tartare Sauce

30 MINS / **SERVES 2**

Who doesn't love fish and chips?! Growing up in Ireland it was always the treat on a Friday night, served in newspaper and eaten on the pier. I don't live by the sea now and so it's become something that I cook at home when I miss Ireland. The batter is light and crisp (make sure the oil is very hot), the chips are crunchy and floury on the inside (I like a Maris Piper potato for these) and there's even a homemade tartare sauce that you can make in under 5 minutes. Hello, Friday!

2 baking potatoes, peeled and cut into 1cm (½in) chips
vegetable oil, for frying
2 thin fillets of cod or haddock, weighing about 140g (5oz) each
2 tablespoons plain flour
sea salt and freshly ground black pepper

For the beer batter
175g (6oz) plain flour
50g (1¾oz) cornflour
½ teaspoon fine salt
1 teaspoon baking powder
285ml (9½fl oz) cold lager

For the tartare sauce
100g (3½oz) mayonnaise
2 tablespoons capers, drained and chopped
2 tablespoons gherkins, drained and chopped
squeeze of lemon juice
1 tablespoon tarragon, finely chopped
1 tablespoon flat-leaf parsley, finely chopped

1. Preheat the oven to 170°C/325°F/gas mark 3.

2. Bring a large pan of salted water to the boil and add the potatoes. Boil for 4 minutes. Drain, pat dry and leave to cool for 5 minutes while you make the beer batter and tartare sauce.

3. For the beer batter, put the flour, cornflour, salt and baking powder in a large bowl and make a well in the middle. Gradually whisk in the lager to make a smooth batter.

4. To make the tartare sauce, combine all the ingredients in a small bowl and season to taste. Set aside.

5. Half-fill a large, heavy-bottomed saucepan big enough to hold the fillets of fish with vegetable oil and heat to 180°C (350°F) – a cube of bread will turn golden in 30 seconds when the oil is hot enough. Once the oil is hot, add the chips and fry for 10 minutes until golden all over. Drain on kitchen paper before transferring to a baking sheet in the oven to keep crisp while you cook the fish.

6. Dust each fish fillet in flour before dipping it into the batter to coat completely. Hold one end of the fish over the batter for a few seconds to allow any excess batter to drip off before gently lowering it into the hot oil. Repeat with the second fillet. Cook for 5–6 minutes, gently flipping the fish halfway through cooking, until the fish is golden, crispy and cooked through. Drain quickly on kitchen paper and serve with the chips, scattered with sea salt, and the tartare sauce alongside.

In Minutes

30 Minutes

Quick Chermoula Fish Parcels

 /

30 MINS / **SERVES 4**

Chermoula (a Moroccan herb marinade used for fish) is unbelievably easy and quick to whip up and makes such a statement of freshness and flavour. All pocketed up in a paper parcel with the fish, chickpeas, red peppers and red onion to create a really healthy supper. This dish looks so good served up in the parcels. If you are looking for something to serve with them, I would suggest basmati rice and grilled chard or broccoli.

400g (14oz) can of chickpeas, drained and rinsed

100g (3½oz) roasted red peppers from a jar, cut into strips

1 small red onion, finely chopped

4 x 150g (5½oz) firm, skinless white fish fillets

For the chermoula

4 tablespoons coriander, chopped

4 tablespoons flat-leaf parsley, chopped

2 garlic cloves, crushed

1 long red chilli, finely chopped

2 tablespoons lemon juice

70ml (2½fl oz) extra virgin olive oil

sea salt and freshly ground black pepper

To serve

rocket

lemon wedges

1. Preheat the oven to 180°C/350°F/gas mark 4. Cut four 30cm (12in) squares of foil and top each with a 15cm (6in) square of baking paper.

2. Start by making the chermoula. Place all the ingredients in a bowl, season with salt and pepper and mix together well.

3. Place the chickpeas, roasted red peppers and red onion in a small bowl and mix together. Divide the chickpea mixture between the paper and foil and top each with a fillet of fish. Spoon one-third of the chermoula over the fish. Fold up the edges of the paper and foil to enclose the fish, scrunching the foil at the top of each parcel to seal. Place the fish parcels on a baking tray and cook in the preheated oven for 15 minutes.

4. Transfer the fish parcels to plates. Open the parcels and spoon the remaining chermoula on top along with some fresh rocket leaves. Serve with a wedge of lemon.

 Cannellini beans would be a good swap for the chickpeas. If you are not a fan of fresh coriander, then you can swap it for fresh mint.

30 Minutes

Crumbed Fish Burgers with Cabbage Slaw

Crispy crumb (using panko breadcrumbs really does make a difference) with a juicy fish fillet inside, then a layer of crunchy fresh slaw and zesty mayo. Sounds like heaven? And these won't take you more than 30 minutes to prepare and cook – hooray! If you don't have coriander, you can use flat-leaf parsley instead and use any white fish you want.

30 MINS / **SERVES 4**

75g (2¾oz) plain flour
1 teaspoon freshly ground black pepper
1 egg, lightly beaten
125g (4½oz) panko breadcrumbs
8 x 100g (3½oz) skinless whiting fillets
sunflower oil, for deep-frying
4 bread rolls, split in half

For the cabbage slaw
160g (5¾oz) shredded red cabbage
160g (5¾oz) shredded green cabbage
1 carrot, grated
2 tablespoons chopped coriander leaves, plus extra leaves to garnish
sea salt and freshly ground black pepper

For the mayo
zest and juice of 1 lemon
1 tablespoon finely chopped coriander
250ml (9fl oz) mayonnaise

1. Start by making the lemon and coriander mayo, just simply mix all the ingredients together in a bowl.

2. For the cabbage slaw, combine the cabbages, carrot and coriander in a bowl with half the mayo. Season, then stir to combine. Set aside until ready to serve.

3. Combine the flour and pepper in a bowl. Place the beaten egg and breadcrumbs in separate bowls. Dip the fish fillets in the flour mixture first, then coat in beaten egg and finally in the breadcrumbs until well coated.

4. Fill a large pan with sunflower oil and heat it to 190°C (375°F) – a cube of bread will turn golden in 30 seconds when the oil is hot enough – then deep-fry the fish, in batches, for 2–3 minutes, or until crisp and golden. Drain on kitchen paper.

5. Serve the fish in rolls with some slaw, the remaining lemon and coriander mayo and extra coriander.

 Haddock and cod are great swaps for the whiting.

Sticky Honey Salmon with Smiling Greens

This dish glows with health on arrival at the table! Sticky, sweet and garlicky, this glazed salmon recipe comes together in just over 20 minutes, and all in one pan. Crunchy sesame seeds add lovely texture and with a fresh, zingy dressing, this recipe is one of my favourite one and done dishes!

30 MINS / **SERVES 4**

200g (7oz) Tenderstem or purple sprouting broccoli
12 asparagus spears, woody ends trimmed
200g (7oz) sugar snap peas
200g (7oz) frozen or fresh peas
1 tablespoon toasted sesame oil
4 salmon fillets
1 tablespoon dark soy sauce
1 tablespoon toasted sesame oil
1 tablespoon honey
2 tablespoons sesame seeds
sea salt

For the dressing
6cm (2½in) piece of fresh ginger, peeled and grated
zest and juice of 2 limes
1 tablespoon toasted sesame oil
3 spring onions, finely chopped
1 red chilli, finely sliced

1. Preheat the oven to 200°C/400°F/gas mark 6.

2. Put the broccoli into a large bowl, cover with boiling water, leave for 1 minute, then drain well.

3. Mix the broccoli, asparagus, sugar snap peas, peas, a pinch of sea salt and the sesame oil in a roasting tin. Put the salmon fillets in around the veg, then mix the soy sauce, sesame oil and honey together and spread over each fillet. Roast for 20 minutes until the salmon is cooked through.

4. Meanwhile, mix together the ginger, lime zest and juice, sesame oil, spring onions and chilli. Once the salmon is cooked, pour the dressing over the vegetables. Scatter over the sesame seeds. Serve hot, with noodles or rice, if you like.

Swap out the asparagus for French beans and the sugar snap peas for kale for a variation.

The Juiciest Burger of All

/

30 MINS / **SERVES 4**

So, what makes it so juicy I hear you ask? Well, it's the combination of the Worcestershire sauce, mayonnaise, sautéed onions and egg yolk, which really does make the patties very juicy and bouncing with flavour. I love to cook these burgers on the barbecue outside even when it's not that warm, they always taste fantastic, but this book is all about ease and speed, so a griddle pan will also work well.

½ tablespoon butter

½ small onion, very finely chopped

1 garlic clove, grated

1 teaspoon thyme leaves, chopped

500g (1lb 2oz) good-quality steak mince

1 teaspoons Dijon mustard

1 teaspoon Worcestershire sauce

1 egg yolk

1 tablespoon full-fat mayonnaise

30g (1oz) fresh breadcrumbs

1 tablespoon olive oil

sea salt and freshly ground black pepper

To serve

4 slices of Emmental or Gruyère cheese

4 brioche burger buns

3 teaspoons Dijon mustard

4 heaped tablespoons mayonnaise

1 small lettuce, leaves separated

2 ripe tomatoes, thickly sliced

a handful of sliced gherkins

1. Melt the butter in a medium frying pan and add the onion, garlic and thyme. Sauté gently for about 5 minutes until the onion is golden and soft.

2. In a large bowl, combine the steak mince, Dijon mustard, Worcestershire sauce, egg yolk, mayonnaise, breadcrumbs and onion mixture. Season liberally with salt and pepper and mix everything together with clean hands. Divide into 4 equal-sized portions and shape into balls, then flatten to make patties the same size as your brioche buns (they will shrink a bit when cooked).

3. Heat the oil in a large, non-stick frying pan over a high heat. Cook the burgers for 4–6 minutes on each side, depending on how rare you like them.

4. Transfer the burgers to a baking tray and top each one with a slice of cheese. Place under a hot grill for 2 minutes until the cheese is melted and bubbling.

5. Toast the brioche buns and mix together the Dijon mustard and mayonnaise, then spread over the inside of the buns. Top with the lettuce, sliced tomatoes, burgers and sliced gherkins.

Chicken Cacciatore

30 MINS / **SERVES 4**

This one-pot supper is just brilliant and a real crowd-pleaser. There are nights (which I am sure you have too), when I just can't bear the idea of washing up more than one pan, so I love a casserole where I can cook it all in one pot. The falling-apart, tender chicken with all the comforting aromatics and Italian flavours of garlic, bay leaf, tomatoes and olives with a bit of chilli heat is just gorgeous. You can serve it up with some rice, roast potatoes or polenta.

---

2 tablespoons olive oil

8 boneless chicken thighs

1 onion, finely chopped

2 garlic cloves, crushed

250ml (9fl oz) red wine (Chianti is good)

1 teaspoon chilli flakes

100ml (3½fl oz) good-quality chicken stock

a handful of pitted black olives

2 x 400g (14oz) cans of plum tomatoes

1 bay leaf

4 sprigs of thyme

2 sprigs of rosemary

400g (14oz) can of cannellini beans, drained and rinsed

sea salt and freshly ground black pepper

1. Heat the oil a large, ovenproof casserole dish or saucepan over a high heat. Season the chicken thighs all over and add to the hot pan. Fry the chicken for 3–4 minutes, turning halfway through cooking until browned on all sides. Remove to a plate.

2. Reduce the heat to medium and add the onion and garlic and fry for 3–4 minutes until golden and soft.

3. Pour in the wine and let it bubble for 1–2 minutes. Return the chicken to the pan and add the chilli flakes, chicken stock, olives, plum tomatoes, bay leaf, thyme and rosemary. Season well and simmer for 15–20 minutes until the chicken is cooked and the sauce has nicely reduced.

4. Stir through the cannellini beans and season with salt and pepper.

Chicken Fajitas

30 MINS / **SERVES 2**

A fantastic, vibrant lift to the midweek supper! I like to serve mine up with a margarita! They are so fun and easy to pull together. I usually put all the fillings in bowls on the table and let everyone help themselves to assembling their own. If you have leftover roast chicken, lamb, beef or pork it will work brilliantly for this recipe.

For the chicken

2 skinless chicken breasts, thinly sliced
1 red pepper, deseeded and thinly sliced
1 small red onion, thinly sliced
1 teaspoon smoked paprika
2 garlic cloves, crushed
1 teaspoon ground cumin
a pinch of mild chilli powder
zest and juice of ½ lime
1 tablespoon olive oil
sea salt and freshly ground black pepper

For the salsa

1 large tomato, chopped
½ small red onion, finely chopped
½ small red chilli, deseeded and finely chopped
2 tablespoons coriander, chopped
juice of 1 lime

To serve

4 small or 2 large flour tortillas
125ml (4fl oz) soured cream
50g (1¾oz) Cheddar cheese, grated
1 ripe avocado, thinly sliced
1 lime, cut into wedges

1. In a large bowl, combine all the ingredients for the chicken, season well and toss until everything is well mixed and the chicken is coated in the spices. Set aside to marinate for 10–15 minutes while you make you the salsa.

2. For the salsa, place the tomato, red onion and chilli in a bowl and season to taste. Add the coriander and lime juice and mix well. Set aside.

3. Heat a griddle pan over a medium heat until hot. Place the chicken, pepper and onion on the griddle and cook for 6–8 minutes or until everything is nicely charred and the chicken is cooked through. Transfer to a warm serving bowl.

4. Briefly place the tortillas on the griddle pan to warm, then serve with the chicken and bowls of soured cream, grated Cheddar, sliced avocado and lime wedges for people to assemble their own fajitas.

If you're looking for a vegetarian or vegan alternative, you could use pan-fried halloumi or tofu.

Creamy Spinach & Ricotta Chicken

Crispy crumb topping, creamy rich ricotta and spinach lying underneath, all adding delicious flavour and texture to the juicy chicken. This is a classic Italian supper and I love serving it with cooked spaghetti that has been tossed in melted butter (or olive oil), lots of freshly ground black pepper and a lovely, fresh green salad.

30 MINS / **SERVES 2**

2 skinless chicken breasts, sliced in half to make 2 thin fillets
1 tablespoon olive oil
20g (¾oz) butter
150g (5½oz) baby spinach
5 tablespoons ricotta
a grating of fresh nutmeg
50g (1¾oz) panko breadcrumbs
50g (1¾oz) Parmesan cheese, finely grated
sea salt and freshly ground black pepper

1. Heat a griddle pan over a medium heat until hot. Brush the chicken with olive oil, season liberally and grill for 3–4 minutes on each side, or until nicely charred and just cooked through.

2. Melt the butter in a large frying pan over a medium heat. Add the spinach and cook until it has just wilted, season with salt and pepper and remove to a plate lined with kitchen paper.

3. Squeeze as much moisture out of the spinach as possible, then roughly chop it and transfer to a bowl. Add the ricotta, a grating of fresh nutmeg and season liberally to taste. Mix well to combine.

4. Once the chicken is cooked, place the fillets on a baking tray and divide the spinach and ricotta mix between the fillets. Spread to cover the tops.

5. Sprinkle over the breadcrumbs and Parmesan and place under a hot grill for 5–6 minutes or until the cheese is melted and the breadcrumbs are toasted.

RECIPE SWAP You can swap the spinach for kale or cavolo nero.

Corn Chowder with Crispy Bacon

30 MINS / **SERVES 4**

This right here is a big bowl of sunshine! It's hearty enough to have as a supper as I've added diced potatoes for more texture and chunkiness. It's really a simple recipe to cook and the ingredients are few and easy to get hold of. Browning the bacon first gives it a smoky flavour base that warms the rest of the chowder. What makes the soup a little thick is the addition of flour and you can use gluten-free flour here too. Serve up with a piece of my Rosemary Clodagh Bread (page 170).

1 tablespoon butter
100g (3½oz) smoked bacon lardons
1 brown onion, finely chopped
1 tablespoon plain flour
450ml (16fl oz) good-quality chicken or vegetable stock
450ml (16fl oz) full-fat milk
2 medium potatoes, peeled and cut into rough 1cm (½in) cubes
½ tablespoon olive oil
4 rashers of smoked streaky bacon
4 spring onions, finely sliced
200g (7oz) frozen or canned sweetcorn, drained if canned
a small bunch of chives, chopped
sea salt and freshly ground black pepper

1. Melt the butter in a large heavy-based saucepan or ovenproof casserole dish over a high heat. Add the bacon lardons and fry for 3–4 minutes until they start to look crispy. Add the onion and fry for a further 3–4 minutes until the onion is beginning to soften.

2. Sprinkle over the flour and mix well to coat the bacon and onion. Pour in the stock and milk and add the potatoes. Bring to a simmer and cook for about 10 minutes until the potatoes are cooked but have not started to fall apart.

3. While the soup is simmering, heat the olive oil in a non-stick frying pan and add the streaky bacon. Fry until very crispy and blot dry on kitchen paper. Set aside.

4. Once the potato is cooked, add the spring onions and sweetcorn to the soup. Bring back up to a simmer to heat the corn through. Season to taste.

5. Ladle the soup into bowls. Break the crispy rashers of bacon into shards and scatter over the soup along with the chopped chives. Garnish with lots of black pepper to serve.

Everyone Loves Spicy Sausage Pasta Bake

I call this 'everyone loves' because this is my most-watched, talked-about and asked-for recipe on Instagram! It's fantastic for feeding a family, and you can make ahead and freeze it too if that works better for you. I will say that having delicious Italian sausages makes such a difference – ones that are either flavoured with fennel, garlic, chilli, oregano or basil.

30 MINS / SERVES 4

2 tablespoons olive oil
1 onion, diced
3 garlic cloves, crushed
8 fresh Italian sausages, cut into
  2.5cm (1in) pieces
400g (14oz) can of chopped
  tomatoes
1 tablespoon tomato purée
2 teaspoons dried oregano, thyme,
  mint, rosemary or fresh basil
1 teaspoon chilli flakes
500g (1lb 2oz) rigatoni, fusilli,
  penne or other bite-sized pasta,
  cooked
100g (3½oz) fresh breadcrumbs
80g (2¾oz) butter, melted
80g (2¾oz) Parmesan, Cheddar or
  any other hard cheese, grated
4 tablespoons ricotta or
  2 mozzarella balls (optional)
sea salt and freshly ground black
  pepper

1. Preheat the oven to 200°C/400°F/gas mark 6.

2. Place a saucepan over a low heat and add 1 tablespoon of olive oil. Stir in the onion, cover and cook for 1 minute, then add the garlic and cook for a further minute. Stir in the sausages and cook for about 5 minutes until they are golden in colour.

3. Pour in the canned tomatoes, then add the tomato purée, herbs and chilli flakes and season with salt and pepper. Stir well and cook for 5 minutes.

4. Stir in the cooked pasta and mix well. Then tip the mixture into a 33 x 23cm (13 x 9in) ovenproof dish.

5. Mix the breadcrumbs with the melted butter and grated cheese. Spoon the breadcrumb mixture on top of the pasta to create a thin layer.

6. If you are adding fresh ricotta or mozzarella, then make little pockets in the pasta and spoon the soft cheese in.

7. Bake in the oven for 15 minutes or until the top is golden.